ROADSIDE ATTRACTIONS

ROADSIDE ATTRACTIONS

cool cafés, souvenir stands, route 66 relics & other road trip fun

BRIAN & SARAH BUTKO

STACKPOLE
BOOKS

*For our parents, Ed and Virginia Link and
Andrew and Dorothy Butko, in thanks for everything*

Published by
STACKPOLE BOOKS
5067 Ritter Road
Mechanicsburg, PA 17055
www.stackpolebooks.com

Printed in China

2 4 6 8 10 9 7 5 3 1

FIRST EDITION

EDITOR: Kyle Weaver
DESIGNER: Beth Oberholtzer

Photos by the authors unless otherwise noted

Frontispiece: Mark Cline gets in the spirit at Foamhenge,
  his creation overlooking U.S. 11, Natural Bridge, Virginia.
This page: Gatorland brochure, c. 1965.

Library of Congress Cataloging-in-Publication Data

Butko, Brian.
    Roadside attractions : cool cafés, souvenir stands, Route 66 relics, and other road
  trip fun / Brian and Sarah Butko. — 1st ed.
        p.   cm.
    Includes bibliographical references and index.
    ISBN-13: 978-0-8117-0229-4 (hardcover)
    ISBN-10: 0-8117-0229-4 (hardcover)
    1. United States—Guidebooks.   2. Roadside architecture—United States—
Guidebooks.   3. Curiosities and wonders—United States—Guidebooks.   4. Automobile travel—United States—Guidebooks.   5. Roads—United States—Guidebooks.
6. United States—History, Local.   I. Butko, Sarah.   II. Title.

E158.B977   2007
917.3'04931—dc22
                                                                2006100610

CONTENTS

INTRODUCTION

HOPING FOR YOUR BUSINESS

A twelve-foot-tall concrete prairie dog watches over the Ranch Store Gift Shop at the eastern end of Badlands National Park, South Dakota. You can visit a colony of these animals out back or another one farther into the park.

Why do people all over the world have such affection for roadside attractions? Goofy monuments, tacky souvenir shops, neon signs that tower over restaurants shaped like sombreros or hot dogs—all have their fans. Tourists make pilgrimages to unique highway markers, mini-golf courses, anything that's the biggest or smallest, and points farthest east, west, north, or south. The automobile era has left a landscape of both thriving and decaying roadside businesses. Some people may call them silly, but others rhapsodize about them, take pictures, and send postcards to friends.

Such places can be new or corporate, but the most revered attractions tend to be one-of-a-kinds from 1920 to 1970. They may show a little wear around the edges, but they maintain a sense of whimsy and reflect the personality of the owners. The best roadside attractions are low-cost or, better yet, free, making the places accessible to all. A good roadside attraction should also have souvenirs—magnets, cups, T-shirts, pennants—that remind us to plan a return trip.

◆ ◆ ◆

Back around 1970, Brian loved visiting his Aunt Em in northern Ohio every summer. (His mom is Dorothy—the kids had a lot of fun with that.) The family loved Cedar Point, when it was still a regional park, and they made side trips to Thomas Edison's birthplace in Milan and the Marblehead

Brian's postcard of Cheese Haven in Marblehead, Ohio. Founded in 1949, the shop offered 88 varieties of cheese for sale. Today, it's up to 125.

peninsula on Lake Erie. A lighthouse, gravity hill, and dinosaur park fueled Brian's imagination. He still has a postcard from Cheese Haven; the out-of-date cars made the image all the more seductive, and to this day, he can't eat smoky cheese without recalling that visit.

For some reason, a visit to The Blue Hole in Castalia is the most vivid. His memories include beekeeping displays, a tiny plate his sister bought, and the bottomless pool of water. But it was the orange late-day sunlight among the trees and the carefree feelings of a summer vacation that left the biggest impression. This blur of happy times spurred a lifetime pursuit into the history and meaning of such places.

Of course, there's the risk that warm recollections will be tarnished by the cold reality of the present. On a recent trip back to Castalia, the beautiful cut stone entrance to The Blue Hole was blocked by warning signs to keep out. Brian attempted to drown his sorrows at the dairy stand across the street, but the workers ranged from sluggish to surly. On the trail of a newer, bigger (bluer?) hole at the nearby state fish hatchery, we

The blue-hued water at The Blue Hole in Castalia, Ohio, could be seen to at least forty-five feet deep. Fish could not live in it because it contained no air, though its outflow fed a brook trout pond. Souvenirs like this are a reminder of the now-closed attraction and childhood visits.

found ourselves at the closed entrance, the hours on the sign different from the dawn to dusk we'd seen online. When we tried to enter, a worker shooed us away. We left town, old memories intact, but new impressions made too. And Brian had no chance of eating his way back to happiness—Cheese Haven was closed that day.

Sarah also took several trips in the early 1970s with her family. Her parents had purchased property near Fort Myers in Lehigh Acres, Florida's first postwar retirement community. They didn't all go on each trip, but usually her older siblings, Debbie, Ralph, and Lester, were along. In the spring of 1974, when Sarah was almost eight years old, she and her family made their first visit to look at the model houses and dream of their future lives. On the drive there and back, the kids always asked to stop at attractions. Sarah remembers being thrilled to walk in the big ring at the Circus Hall of Fame in Sarasota. At Larry's Safari in Naples, getting so close to alligators was something she hadn't done before. And seeing the pink signs for Chico's Monkey Farm in Georgia made her wonder what monkeys were doing on a farm, so she couldn't wait to see that place. Although she'd seen many animals at her local zoo, there was just something special about *these* animals.

Like the places in Brian's childhood, few have survived intact. The Circus Hall of Fame, founded in 1857 to honor legendary circus artists, was attracting 80,000 visitors a year in 1979 when the land it leased was sold. The residents of Peru, Indiana, raised funds to purchase the museum's contents and bring it to their town. Now the expanded collection includes more than forty vintage circus wagons and steam calliopes, costumes, props, and posters.

Larry's Safari started in 1919 as the botanical gardens of Dr. Henry Nahrling. By 1950, with the land in disrepair, Julius Fleischmann, grandson of the man who pioneered Fleischmann Yeast, began restoring the site. Adding birds, lakes, and plants, he opened it in 1954 as Caribbean Gardens. In 1969, new owners Col. Lawrence and Nancy Jane Tetzlaff, known as Jungle Larry and Safari Jane, renamed the place Jungle Larry's

Sarah visits Chico's in Richmond Hill, Georgia.

African Safari and began animal shows and exhibits. We both remember their second, northern location—the Jungle Larry's at Cedar Point. It closed after thirty years in 1994, and at the same time, the Florida location reverted to Caribbean Gardens. Jane remains active there along with sons David and Tim. Reflecting its growth, the site has *again* been renamed and is now Naples Zoo at Caribbean Gardens.

Chico's was located on U.S. Route 17 in Richmond Hill, Georgia, about twenty-five miles south of Savannah. It was run by Bobby Snowden, former manager of the King Brothers Circus, and was staffed by his carny friends. After I-95 opened, the place declined and finally closed in the early 1980s. It has been memorialized in a song called "Chico's Monkey Farm" on the 1993 album *Funzo's Knuckle Room* by the LaBrea Stompers and in a recent short-story collection by Kenneth R. Fussell titled *Chico's Monkey Farm; and Other Southern Tales*. But all that remains of this once-thriving attraction is scattered clues and a few online recollections.

Both our families visited the opening season of Sea World Ohio in 1970. Brian's dad, especially, had always taken the family to the openings of new attractions. Two years later, they were in Orlando for the first season of Walt Disney World, which had opened in October 1971. This giant

Mission Village, Los Angeles, as portrayed on its letterhead. KEITH SCULLE

The road from Sacramento to San Francisco was, in the 1950s, just a narrow highway with little to see along the way besides cows grazing on the rolling hills and a fruit stand in the shape of an orange. The Giant Orange, as it was called, was the highlight of the trip in my ten-year-old mind, but it was a story my father told me about the cows that stays with me today. You see, the cows all seemed to face the same direction as they grazed, a circumstance made possible, Dad assured me, because they'd been born with their uphill legs shorter than their downhill ones.

—JAN FRIEDMAN, author of *Eccentric America*

theme park turned out to be the biggest boon ever to Florida tourism, but it drew many tourists away from the old parks. With the gas crisis hitting two years later, owners who were pondering retirement had to close their doors.

◆ ◆ ◆

The oddball, over-the-top places we love are mostly found along old two-lane roads, known better for their names than their numbers, such as the Lincoln Highway, Dixie Highway, or Old Span-

After millennia as home to Native Americans, the Black Hills of South Dakota saw a rush of fortune seekers after the discovery of gold in 1870. By the twentieth century, the towering granite peaks covered in ponderosa pine drew automobile tourists to the area.

ish Trail. Along with these better-known routes are dozens more, such as the Mohawk Trail in New England, the Yellowstone Trail across the North, the Jefferson Highway down through the central United States, the Ozark Trail across the Southwest, the Redwood Highway in the Pacific Northwest, and the Going-to-the-Sun Road through Glacier National Park. Any of the numbered federal highways established in the 1920s are likewise lined with reminders of an earlier era of travel, among them U.S. Routes 6, 11, 20, 40, 80, 89, 101, and the famed 66. These and many more have devoted fans. One family we met started following entire routes in numeric order three decades ago, starting with U.S. 1 the first year, U.S. 2 the following year, and so on, seeing lots of the country along the way.

Even before the auto, travelers were stopping at natural wonders, usually odd land or water formations like Niagara Falls, Devil's Tower in Wyoming, the giant rock formations in Utah's Arches National Park, or the many show caverns across the country. In the early twentieth century, the automobile brought tourist services to the open road. By the 1920s, towns that begged for tourist traffic a decade earlier began building bypasses to ease congestion. With straighter roads and faster cars, signs grew larger and more flashy—and the ultimate sign in some cases was the building itself. A whole architectural genre of buildings-as-things arose, best remembered by giant coffeepot cafés or pig-

Like many drive-ins of the 1940s and early 1950s, the El Patio in Cairo, Illinois, had a concrete screen that also served as a giant advertisement for the theater.

shaped diners. After World War II, the exodus to the new suburbs brought drive-in restaurants, theaters, pharmacies, and any other businesses that could be adapted to a mobile clientele.

Shopping centers were partly meant to be an antidote to the increasingly crowded, auto-oriented roadscape. Customers could again walk between stores. But getting to them still meant driving, and they quickly became crowded and cluttered. With the rise of interstate highways and suburban development many miles from city centers, the old strips declined, attracting fewer customers but more crime and litter.

A few of the vintage attractions moved to exit ramps or, if they survived in place, became time warps with less revenue available for remodeling. It's that patina of old places that road fans and even the general public finds so alluring. Even if most people vacation at Disney, they'll try a classic attraction for old times' sake.

The Pop Art movement and the rise of franchises in the 1960s inspired artists and writers to document the disappearing roadside culture. One of the earliest books to cover the roadside spec-

trum was Jane and Michael Stern's *Amazing America*, published in 1977, a concise yet comprehensive collection of oddities from Cadillac Ranch to the Largest Ball of Twine. A decade later, the authors of *Roadside America* really enlivened appreciation for the offbeat.

Mid-twentieth-century travel was less fun for minorities. This cabin camp in western North Carolina made clear that its "nice" offerings were "restricted."

5

When I was very little, my mom used two service stations. The attendants knew her and her charming way. I always liked their friendly banter, the odor of Ethyl fumes filling her 1941 Oldsmobile four-door fastback sedan, and the routine of getting my mom's car serviced. I loved the dance.

We'd pass other stations along the usual routes, and I enjoyed distinguishing the various logos and their graphics: the round Gulf sign, the flying red horse Pegasus for Mobil, the blue-and-white circle for Pure Oil, the H-C dinosaur, Amoco's oval stripes, and the simple letter-formed Standard sign where my mom had her Olds catered to, ration stamps and all.

One service station stood out from those we passed every week. My eyes throbbed, but my mom would never stop because she had brand loyalty and was a devoted customer to the Standard stations. But I still clearly recall the iceberg station on Piedmont Avenue in Atlanta, Georgia. Oh, how I loved its unique architecture, and I wondered what went on inside. Was it different from the usual gas stations?

Years later, when my roadside postcard collection started to gain momentum, I had a card of a similar station out west. I loved it so much that I paid homage to my Atlanta memories and did a watercolor from the image.

—JOHN BAEDER, artist and author of *Gas, Food and Lodging: A Postcard Odyssey through the Great American Roadside*

Col. Poole's Pig Hill of Fame, East Ellijay, Ga., by John Baeder, oil on canvas, 44 x 66 inches, 1995.

The definition of a roadside attraction is broad. We might think of famous entertainment venues, but also included are old motels, diners, dairy stands—anywhere that bespeaks a slower time, often with more personal service. A few, such as Wall Drug and South of the Border, started along two-lane highways and have grown with the interstates. Others blossomed when ambitious operators kept expanding, but then faded for various reasons. A couple miles north of Cairo, Illinois, Fred Sullivan built a roadside empire along the Ohio River where S.R. 3 met U.S. 51. His El Patio complex included a café featuring the popular trio of the day, steak, chicken, and frog legs; a bar and grill that hosted big-name bands; a drive-in theater; free pony rides; Roller Bowl skating rink; a Phillips 66 station; Cairo Motel, with twenty-six rooms plus six cottages; and even an adjacent Pepsi-Cola plant. Only tattered remnants survive, less than a mile from I-57. Early chain businesses also fall into this category, and fans search out the ones with old

design elements that are still in use, such as KFC restaurants with pole-top buckets, giant neon Arby's hats, single-arch McDonald's signs, and the Phillips 76 big orange balls.

Few gas stations were built as tourist attractions, but some sported outrageous designs to capture people's attention and thus a few extra tourist dollars. Even most pre-1980 corporate stations are now shuttered, spurring interest in adapting them to other uses, and fortunately, historic preservation tax incentives are available for restorations. A station on Pittsburgh's South Side has recently been redone as the Double Wide Grill, sporting petroliana decor. On the Dixie Highway in Cartersville, Georgia, an old Pure Oil Service Station was restored, only to be demolished later. Another Pure Oil station in McMinnville, Tennessee, is now used as an art gallery. The owners of Tangletown Gardens nursery in Minneapolis, Minnesota, adapted a blue-roofed Pure Oil station into a centerpiece of their business. A 1922 Standard Service Station has been restored as an information center in Port Huron, Michigan. In Milwaukee, Wisconsin, a Streamline Moderne station now houses Sherman Perk, serving food and locally roasted coffee. In Tazewell, Tennessee, on a bypassed segment of U.S. 25, a branch of the Dixie Highway, the 1930 Rose Service Station was restored by townspeople in 2001 and serves as a small petroliana museum. Reed's Standard Service Station in Colo, Iowa, is similarly a showcase for artifacts of early auto travel. The adjacent Niland's Café and Colo Motel were part of the town-led revival of this one-stop, offering gas, food, and lodging at the intersection of the Lincoln and Jefferson Highways.

People are drawn to places that are the largest or farthest. In Yarmouth, Maine, at the headquarters of DeLorme mapping products, the World's Largest Revolving and Rotating Globe was unveiled in 1998 after two years of work. Eartha is 41.5 feet in diameter, includes 3-D landforms, and has two motors that make it revolve and rotate once each minute. In Queens, New York, Flushing Meadows Corona Park was the

This Art Deco Signal gas station in Portland, Oregon, now pumps out pizza. ANDREW AND JENNY WOOD

A Pure Oil cottage-style station was restored on the Dixie Highway in Cartersville, Georgia, shown here around 1995, but was demolished by 2006. JEFFREY L. DURBIN

A road trip down U.S. 1 isn't complete until you reach the Southernmost Point marker, shaped like a concrete buoy, at Mile 0 in Key West, Florida. O'DEA FAMILY

to serve other attractions. Fiberglass Animals, Shapes and Trademarks makes giant cows, dolphins, and a hundred other fun figures. Scattered in the field around the company's workshops are many samples and the molds for all these creatures. A sign invites visitors to look around—but don't touch.

Natural Bridge, Virginia, is another locus for fiberglass fun, with the facilities of Enchanted Castle Studios. Here madcap creator Mark Cline makes dragons, monsters, skeletons, and any other creature that customers request—or that enters his mind. After a late-night fire, apparently aimed at ending his "weird" vocation, destroyed the site, Cline rebuilt his workshop and has now developed several new outlets for entertaining people through surreal experiences. He appears gentle but then slips into the role of one of the characters who inhabit his walk-through attraction, Professor Cline's Haunted Monster Museum. Just out the front door is his Escape from Dinosaur King-

site of the New York World's Fair for 1939–40 and 1964–65. Most visitors go there to see the stainless steel Unisphere from the latter fair—at 140 feet tall, it's the largest representation of the earth ever made. It was an engineering challenge to make this open sculpture able to withstand rain, ice, and the area's salty gales.

Certain incidental locations become attractions because of their historic or cultural value. Four decades of tourists have congregated at the intersection of San Francisco's Haight and Ashbury Streets, locus of the hippie movement. By 1965, groups like the Jefferson Airplane and Grateful Dead were settling into unwanted Victorian houses, and word spread that it was *the* place for psychedelics. By 1967, carfuls and busloads of teens from across the country arrived daily, while Middle America came to gawk and insult. If they bought anything, it was a poster of the already famous street signs.

Businesses like F.A.S.T in Sparta, Wisconsin, have become attractions, even though they're there

Every few minutes, camera-toting tourists—like us—make their way to the corner of Haight and Ashbury Streets in San Francisco.

dom, where Union Civil War soldiers have stumbled upon the prehistoric beasts to predictable, and comic, results. Just north stands one of his flashes of creativity, Foamhenge, an exact Styrofoam replica of the more famous Stonehenge, this one installed overnight as an April Fool's prank in 2004.

In recent years, roadside attractions have reached a level of public appreciation that was unimaginable a generation ago. They've become cool across generations. States like Nebraska have added categories to their websites listing attractions such as Carhenge near Alliance or the World's Largest Porch Swing in Hebron. Even Weird Al Yankovic penned an ode to roadside attractions, "The Biggest Ball of Twine in Minnesota," an original song for his 1989 *UHF* motion picture soundtrack. That twine ball, in the town of

Darwin, indeed is signed as the "World's Largest Twine Ball," but right in the middle is the fine print "by 1 man." Francis A. Johnson spun it from 1950 until his death in 1989, when the 17,400-pound ball was moved by the city into a gazebo downtown. The result of all this attention was that it spurred others to compete, hence a bigger twine ball still being spun in Cawker City, Kansas.

Keith Holt and his wife Diane Karnes have even gone so far as to purposely create a roadside attraction. They're converting their family property south of Paducah, Kentucky, into the Historic Apple Valley Roadside Attraction. There's an Old West store, a fake roadside zoo, and Hillbilly Garden, which includes Lawnmower Ranch, a homage to Texas's Cadillac Ranch. Holt has also been inspired by Tinkertown in New Mexico and is building similar projects with bottles.

Since the 1970s, authors and artists have attempted to document, promote, and profit from these places. Libraries and archives were slow to respond but increasingly collect post–World War II images and histories. Some 75,000 photographs and a massive collection of ephemera from photographer John Margolies may end up at the Prints and Photographs Division of the Library of Congress. Websites, too, catalog seemingly endless

No, Mr. Bendo is not sweating; it's just a rainy day at Ralph's Mufflers in Indianapolis, three miles east of the Indianapolis Motor Speedway. Today such Muffler Men are sought after and cataloged by legions of fans.

roadside oddities and document favorites, such as Muffler Men, the fiberglass giants that once advertised auto repair shops along the road. Most of them have been converted to other duties with various costumes and poses, such as the cowboy at Cowtown Rodeo in New Jersey or the Gemini astronaut at the Launching Pad Café in Illinois.

That's not to say the threat of their disappearance has passed. Indeed, a startling number of roadside attractions have closed in recent years, usually for the same reasons—changing tastes and valuable land needed for other purposes. The past few years have been especially bad for classic parks.

In New York, the Catskill Game Farm had entertained since 1933. It had grown to some 2,000 exotic animals from around the world, with petting areas, amusement rides, and a half-mile train ride. But in late 2006, the park closed. Owner Kathie Schulz, daughter of the founders, said that attendance just could not keep up with the demands of the park. TV and the Internet have made seeing live animals obsolete, plus kids and parents expect modern entertainment, such as water slides and thrill rides. Animal regulations became another obstacle. One of the rides up for auction was a thirty-horse carousel that the farm bought new in 1951.

Roadside culture also spread across Canada, Mexico, and even overseas: Sunnyside Beach Park in Toronto, Canada, was a resort along Lake Ontario for seventy years before an amusement park opened there in 1922. Seen here a year later are the Flyer roller coaster and the entrance to Fun Land at right. Land reclamation allowed the park to grow, but it remained split by two major roads. That danger, along with traffic congestion, led to the park's demolition after the 1955 season for the Gardiner Expressway. Twelve lanes of traffic plus rail lines now cover the site, though the bathing pavilion remains. MIKE FILEY COLLECTION

In Minnesota, the Paul Bunyan Amusement Park along Lake Bemidji, opened in 1960, was auctioned after the 2006 season. The owner was nearing retirement and sold the amusement rides but is keeping a mini-golf course and little train ride until the land lease expires in 2010. There were other auctions that same fall for Santa's Village Amusement Park in Dundee, Illinois, outside Chicago; Erieview Park in Geneva-on-the-Lake, Ohio; and the Pavillion in Myrtle Beach, South Carolina. The previous season saw the permanent shuttering of Libertyland on Early Maxwell Boulevard in Memphis, Elvis's favorite, which he occasionally rented out at night or reserved for Lisa Marie's parties.

In Atlantic Beach, North Carolina, a fishing pier and two campgrounds nestled in the sand dunes were demolished in 2006 to make room for high-rise condos. While places like the eleven-unit Sand Dollar Motel still go for $400 a week, new condos start at $900,000. The Circle, which offered locals a pavilion, arcades, and rides, is being replaced by The Grove commercial and residential complex, with three condo buildings at least fifteen stories high. Jungleland Amusement Park, a few miles away on West Fort Megan Road, nonetheless had its contents auctioned so the land could be redeveloped. Nostalgia pales when landowners are offered millions of dollars for their prime real estate.

Fortunately, some attractions relocate. In Aspen Park, Colorado, the owners of a hot-dog-shaped diner put it up for sale when they decided to sell the land. If the hot dog was to survive, new owners would have to move it. The place had been conceived decades ago to be the first in a chain of hot-dog-shaped stands. Named the Boardwalk at Coney Island, it opened its doors at 4190 West Colfax Avenue in July 1966 but closed within two years and was removed to a mobile-home lot in Lakewood. It sat there another two years, then was moved southwest to Aspen Park, where it reopened on June 4, 1970, the name changed to Coney Island Dairy Land. Though locals at first bristled against such an oddity, they came to embrace it and waved good-bye tearfully when it

El Peñon had twenty-four tourist cabins, a bar, and an "ultra modern spacious" restaurant on the highway between Laredo and Mexico City. The senders of this card called it a "hair raising drive" with "hair pin curves" but "wonderful scenery."

was again moved. The big dog was hauled twenty miles away in March 2006, settling on a spot about half a mile south of Bailey. When we visited that summer, Ron Aigner and Diane Wiescamp were working on multiple parts of the site so the hot dog can reopen, along with a dining area and even some overnight accommodations. How did Ron come to own it? He was driving the train at nearby Tiny Town and informed the owners that the hot dog was up for sale, thinking it would be a nice match to the park's miniature version. When they weren't interested, he and Diane snapped it up.

Tiny Town itself has entertained travelers since 1920 with an assortment of one-sixth-size buildings and a miniature steam locomotive. Various calamities have befallen the park, causing it to close numerous times, but in 1988, volunteers refurbished the structures. Two years later, a foundation was created to make it a non-profit venture.

Running such attractions can be difficult; trying to sell them can be nearly impossible. A site where the owner does every job, all day long, every day of the year, is a tough sell to generations raised on working one job for others.

In Yeehaw Junction, Florida, $2.8 million will purchase the Desert Inn and Restaurant, but the only interested buyer wants to bulldoze it. Owner

The Pizza House on Highway 1 in Ginowan City, Japan, specialized in Italian cuisine.

Beverly Zicheck rejected the offer and continues to carry on in the restaurant, where she serves up such old-time Florida favorites as frogs, catfish, and gator burgers. For $4.95, the 3^1/$_2$-ounce gator burger comes in a basket with fries or cole slaw. A dollar more gets you a turtle burger. Stay late and you can have a room for $33.90. Founded in 1889, the complex is in the National Register of Historic Places and was renowned for raising jackasses, hence the town's name. But what was once a rural outpost now has, among other neighbors, the newly developed city of Destiny, with an anticipated population of 75,000. Chances are, most of those new homeowners will choose chain restaurants over an offbeat, old-fashioned eatery with character.

◆ ◆ ◆

We've traveled a lot of the country over the years, stopping at many attractions and photographing them. But for all we've seen, thousands more places are waiting. We made it to Oahu, Hawaii, and though we weren't hunting roadside attractions, we did hit many of the standard tourist stops. We loaded up on souvenirs at the International Marketplace, developed in 1955 by the founder of Don the Beachcomber Polynesian-style restaurants. With real estate at a premium, there were recent plans to demolish and rebuild the site, but they've been scaled back to a renovation. On the north end of the island, we saw the cliff-diving show at Waimea Falls Park. The site has been remade as Waimea Valley Audubon Center, lush with tropical plants but no more diving or hula displays. We haven't made it to Alaska, but there are a number of places we'd like to see, such as a four-story, igloo-shaped hotel. It never opened—the builder couldn't bring himself to add fire escapes to its cool exterior—so it's sat empty for three decades. It's going to be a long drive, but we'll see it someday.

We often ask our friends about places they like. That spawned one of our favorite features of this book, the Fan Favorites, written by others who have been there. Some penned touching stories about their memories from childhood trips. Others wrote glowingly of places still in business. It's great fun reading all of them.

We make no attempt with this book to be comprehensive—each state alone would have dozens of entries. Books like *Eccentric America* and a number of series with words such as "Oddball," "Curiosities," or "Weird" in the title cover attractions state-by-state. But as with *Roadside Giants*, our intent is to be inspirational, not inclusive. So when you plan your trip, we hope you'll visit the places mentioned here. Even better, we hope you'll visit lots more.

SPOTLIGHT ON
Drive-In Theaters

Millions love them, many lament their demise, yet drive-ins continue to fall to development every year. The novelty of watching movies from one's car was enhanced in the 1950s by drive-ins offering playgrounds, bottle warmers, ponies, and miniature trains. By the 1970s, however, the novelty had worn off and cable was bringing movies into the home. From a peak of some 4,000 in 1958, only a tenth survive, and at the end of each summer, a few more go dark. Some sit empty or are later revived, but most make way for shopping centers or housing.

One such site is near Cleveland, Ohio. The Miles, with its streamlined tower, operated from 1953 until September 2000; then its 1,000 spaces lay fallow until recently, when plans were announced for 100 houses. The development, Cinema Park, will have model houses named for famous films and streets named for movie stars.

According to the United Drive-In Theatre Owners Association (UDITOA), sixty-three drive-ins have reopened since the 1990s (though nine closed again), and an amazing forty have been built (though six of those closed too). Nine of those new builds have been in Alabama. The Harpersville Drive-In, named after its Alabama location, opened at the site of a former flea market in June 2006, with town leaders hoping it might bring more business and residents fearing the increase of speeding traffic on U.S. 280. The price is definitely right at the Harpersville's two screens: $10 per car, half price on Wednesdays.

When Hull's Drive-In closed in Lexington, Virginia, townsfolk were determined to hang on to the family-friendly resource. After lots of $5 and $10 donations, the theater is now community-owned. With double fea-

Sunset at the Motor Vu in Parma, Idaho. Note the little car painted above the marquee. DOUGLAS TOWNE

tures just $5 for adults and free for kids, the lot once again fills on warm nights.

Tulsa's Admiral Twin Drive-In is among the two dozen grant winners of Hampton Inns' Save-A-Landmark program, which funds improvements to roadside attractions. The 1951 theater is best known for its role in Francis Ford Coppola's *The Outsiders*, based on the novel by Tulsa native S. E. Hinton.

In Hockley, Texas, bankers thought that brothers Chris and John Rumfolo were crazy to plan a new drive-in, but on opening day in spring 2006, the Showboat Drive-In had to turn cars away.

Still, it's always tempting for owners of these lots to sell to a developer for a lump sum versus facing the time, labor, and upkeep necessary to run a vintage drive-in year after year. At the Memphis Drive-In Theater southwest of Cleveland, rumors had floated for years that the three-screen site had been sold. This 1954 theater was one of the last to maintain its original

Shankweiler's Drive-In Theatre in Orefield, Pennsylvania, is the oldest operating drive-in. It was actually the second one ever when it opened on April 15, 1934, less than a year after Richard Hollingshead pioneered the concept in Camden, New Jersey. Paul Geissinger began working at the theater in 1971 and he and his wife, Susan, bought it in 1984.

The Bengies Drive-In in Baltimore. The marquee is a 1973 update of the original. KEN ADAM

speakers, but it closed at the end of 2006 and was sold to the American Greeting Card Company.

Regulars at Detroit's Ford-Wyoming Drive-In have the same fear. Signs along Wyoming Avenue in summer 2006 advertised fourteen acres for sale. The owner explained that he leases that land for screens six through nine, which can be sold, but he owns the land along Ford Road that holds screens one through five. These five screens are open all year—in-car heaters are offered in winter. Opened with one screen in 1950, it remains prosperous, but of the thirty-some drive-ins that flourished in Detroit in the 1960s, this is the sole survivor.

At the Columbia Drive-In, the last in Lancaster County, Pennsylvania, the owners lost their lease and had to close after the 2005 season. Despite 20,000 signatures on a petition against it, the land was cleared. That's the common theme played out over the past three decades. After all, drive-ins make money only a few hours per night, mostly on weekends, and are usually closed between Labor Day and Memorial Day.

Yet many hang on and prosper. The Swap Shop Drive-In in Fort Lauderdale, Florida, opened as the Thunderbird Drive-In with one screen in November 1963. Weekend flea markets began in 1966, and the eighty-eight-acre lot has grown to include carnival rides, a video arcade, food court, and fourteen screens.

One of the best known is the Bengies, near Baltimore, which has the biggest screen in the United States. The theater is named for its neighborhood. Jack Vogel, the step-father of owner D. Vogel, was an architect-engineer who designed more than 300 drive-ins. He built this one to run himself and opened it on June 6, 1956. One regular customer was a young John Waters, who later honored the drive-in by filming *Cecil B. Demented* (2000) here.

The Bengies is almost completely restored and still sports a vintage swing set. The rows are double ramped so that instead of one car per row, there are two with bumpers nearly touching. For half a century, the National Anthem has been played at the start of each everning's screening. The projectors roll nonstop, playing cartoons and vintage trailers with dancing food advertising concessions between the features. Theaters make their profit at the snack bar, and we patrons are always happy to help.

FAN FAVORITE

When I drove back and forth from my home in Pennsylvania to school in upstate New York, my favorite landmark was the Comerford Drive-In Theatre, located on Route 315 just off the interstate between Scranton and Wilkes-Barre. The marquee had little neon cars running sequentially across the top of the signboard, and I would pull off the road just to watch them skip along. By the time the theater was torn down, I had finished school and no longer traveled that route regularly. I'm glad I didn't have to witness that sad sight, but at least we were able to salvage the letters.

—REBECCA SHIFFER, past president of the Society for Commercial Archeology

The Comerford in Dupont, Pennsylvania, opened in 1955 and closed less than thirty years later.

CHAPTER 1
FAMILIAR FAVORITES

The Corn Palace in Mitchell, South Dakota.

When certain places are mentioned, they produce a knowing look. People remember them, either from their own childhood or their own experiences with kids in the backseat—"Can we stop? Please, *please*, can we stop?" Some of these places are individual attractions, like Roadside America. Others are entire towns, usually considered vacation resort areas, like Myrtle Beach. Let's take a look at both kinds.

Two of the best-known individual attractions are Wall Drug and South of the Border. If you've driven in the Midwest or along the Mid-Atlantic coast, you've seen their billboards, dozens of them, many starting hundreds of miles away. Fans of Wall Drug have even mounted signs overseas. South of the Border sells a booklet of its most memorable billboards, such as "You Never Sausage a Place." Lots of parents refuse to be drawn into these "tourist traps," which tells us they are good roadside attractions.

Wall Drug says that 20,000 visitors stop by on a hot day for the free ice water that is advertised on their signs or to browse the acres of artifacts, souvenirs, and amusements. They come to see the *Jurassic Park* T-rex roaring for the crowds or the giant jackalope, which every kid wants to climb. This attraction really did start out as a drugstore in the tiny prairie town of Wall, South Dakota. In a 1982 *Guideposts* magazine article, Ted Hustead recalled that in 1936, after five years of struggling, his wife, Dorothy, suggested that free ice water might draw in some of the cars whizzing by. "I went out to the highway and put up our signs for free ice water. I must admit that I felt somewhat silly doing it, but by the time I got back to the store, people had already begun showing up for their ice water. Dorothy was running all around to keep up." By the following summer, they had eight young women helping them. The business has grown ever since and now includes the third generation of Husteads.

Inside, the main hall looks like a compact western townscape, with facades of native timber and old brick and a street made of Cheyenne river rock. At every counter, you'll find a stack of bumper stickers; Wall Drug learned long ago the value of free publicity. They give away about 14,000 of these little signs every year plus another 8,000 larger ones, and there are also the billboards lining hundreds of miles of roadway and elsewhere around the world. Towering over the interstate, in case you miss the signs, is an eighty-foot-tall dinosaur.

Most visitors to Wall are headed to the Black Hills to visit Mount Rushmore or the even larger Crazy Horse Memorial, started in 1948 as a trib-

Main Street in the little town of Wall, South Dakota.

ute to the Lakota warrior. Tourist businesses sprang up decades ago, and many survive, such as the National Museum of Woodcarving, Bear Country U.S.A., and Reptile Garden, where you can see a rabbit shoot a ping-pong-ball gun or a chicken play poker—though both had better watch out for those reptiles.

It's no coincidence that roadside attractions thrive in the Midwest—tourists have spent a century crossing the Great Plains, heading west on vacation or east to the big cities. Especially now interstates keep drivers from seeing anything but chain restaurants at exit ramps. The only way to pull potential customers off the four-lane is to advertise something outrageous. From Wisconsin to the Dakotas and down through Kansas, you'll find tractor museums, 5¢ coffee, antique malls, Indian crafts, and the world's largest anything.

There are numerous replicas of Stonehenge, the mysterious monoliths atop Great Britain's Salisbury Plain, but only in Alliance, Nebraska, will you find it re-created with thirty-eight automobiles. The idea came to Jim Reinder, who studied the original while living in England. At a wake for his father in 1982, he proposed it as a memorial. His family agreed to meet again in five years to build it. On the summer solstice of 1987, they dedicated the gray-painted ring of cars with songs, poems, and a play. The city council soon wanted the "junk" torn down, but others realized its role as folk art and as a tourist attraction. A group called Friends of Carhenge now owns and maintains the site, which has grown to include other outdoor art.

Like Carhenge, the Corn Palace in Mitchell, South Dakota, is yet another midwestern attempt to lure travelers off the interstate. The exterior of the building is covered every year with corncob halves. Colored varieties are grown specifically to allow the creation of murals. The one in 2006 was a salute to rodeo. Decorating with corncobs was once a common way for rural towns to showcase their crops and the fertility of their soil. The first palace here was built in 1892. The third and present building is made of concrete and was completed in 1921; its Moorish domes and minarets

were added in 1937. The Corn Palace hosts stage shows and sporting events.

South of the Border similarly began as a simple endeavor spurred to fame and fortune by a gimmick, this one its name. Alan Schafer built a beer stand on a main north-south Atlantic coast route in 1949. Located near Dillon, South Carolina, just across the state line from North Carolina's dry counties, he named it South of the Border Beer Depot. Success brought the addition of a restaurant and motel, and Shafer began importing gift-shop merchandise from Mexico to play on the name. South of the Border has grown to include a small amusement park, arcades, mini-golf, the 200-foot-tall Sombrero Tower, campground, drug store, candy shop, fireworks store, and wedding chapel. It still sprawls across U.S. 301 and 501, but most traffic speeds by now on I-95, which is famously lined with dozens of SOTB billboards. Pedro, the mascot, is everywhere, portrayed on many statues and signs. The largest sign overlooks the interstate and is lit by nearly 25,000 bulbs. Mexican food is available at South of the Border and many travelers make a

It feels like only yesterday. The sky was blue and all was right with the world. We'd packed our dogs and our fishing poles and our camping gear and drove from Denver to Alliance, Nebraska, and then we drove two miles more. We arrived at our fabled destination—Carhenge—and wandered through the tattered gray ring made of American automobiles, a scale model of Stonehenge with AMC Gremlins and Cadillacs for stones. A Japanese tourist was there. "Why?" she asked.

We had no answer. Later I learned the origin of the postmodern replica: It was "something to do" at the Reinders family reunion in 1987, fueled by cosmic inspiration, hard work, and cold beer.

—ERIC PETERSON, author of *Ramble: A Field Guide to the U.S.A.* and *Roadside Americana*

Most famous of the American Stonehenge re-creations is Carhenge, just north of Alliance, Nebraska. On this sunny day, Liz Ahl photographed friends Sandy Yannone and Sherrie Flick. Sandy and Liz are poets. Sherrie, a fiction writer, says, "Poets just love Carhenge. It's so strange and ironic and yet pastoral. Every time I went there while I was in grad school (and that was once a year), it was with a carload of poets." LIZ AHL

than 900 barns throughout the South. But in the 1960s, the highway beautification movement reduced them to fewer than 100.

The attraction was started as a rock garden by Garnet and Frieda Carter, who had developed exclusive housing atop Lookout Mountain in 1924. To appease new residents of Fairyland, waiting for their promised golf course, the Carters built what is believed to have been the first miniature golf, Tom Thumb Golf, which they later franchised. With the onset of the Depression, the Carters developed the rock garden as a source of income, creating winding, enchanting paths lined with more than 400 plant species and statuary, mostly gnomes. Near the end, strollers enter Fairyland Caverns and Mother Goose Village, where

Gift shops and snack stands are a big part of South of the Border near Dillon, South Carolina.

point of picking up some Blenheim Ginger Beer, a spicy regional beverage.

Rock City is fondly known for its barn-side advertisements. The site made agreements with farmers to paint their barns in exchange for using one side of the structure as a billboard. The words "See Rock City," therefore, were painted on more

fairy tales are depicted with glowing backlight. The third generation now operates the popular attraction. Vintage motels are found throughout the area, such as the pre–World War II Chanticleer Inn, located just outside Rock City.

A fourth attraction known for its signage is Harold Warp's Pioneer Village, which covers twenty acres and two city blocks in tiny Minden, Nebraska, at U.S. 6 and 34. Most signs line I-80, beckoning travelers to "See How America Grew" and boasting exhibits of "Everything Used by the Average Person Since 1830." The signs are true— there are endless buildings housing every invention and contraption imaginable. The objects are arranged in chronological order, so whether your interest is steam tractors or dolls or TVs or even kitchens over time, you'll find them here. It was founded in 1953 by Harold Warp, who made a fortune in plastics. The actual idea had come six years earlier, when the little school he'd attended as a child was put up for sale. The dozen buildings encircling the village green are artifacts too, from a sod house and frontier fort to the requisite church and general store. The site also holds a motel, campground, and restaurant. The entire

A vintage souvenir plate from Rock City, along the Tennessee-Georgia border.

complex, including Warp plastics, is now run by Warp's son, Harold G. Warp.

Hosting far fewer billboards, but just as beloved, is Roadside America in southeastern Pennsylvania. Opened in 1953 along old U.S. 22,

A wagon with its top edge painted blue to resemble the sky sits atop the entrance to Harold Warp's Pioneer Village, Minden, Nebraska.

it now faces the four-lane I-78/U.S. 22 but is fenced off from it, making what was once an impulse stop now an interstate exit trip. Still, lots of people take the time to enter past the Pennsylvania Dutch Gift Haus and a giant fiberglass Amish couple atop a towing trailer. Inside is a wonderland of 300 miniature buildings and 4,000 figures intermixed with running trains and trolleys. The O-gauge layout was started in 1935 at the home of Lawrence Gieringer, who recalled that as children, he and his brother thought far-

Kids young and old like to push the buttons for animating the scenes at Roadside America, Shartlesville, Pennsylvania. ANDREW AND JENNY WOOD

away places really were that small. This was his homage to that world, and his wife helped too, making some 10,000 trees and bushes. It moved into the current building in 1941. Gieringer continued working on his project until his death in 1963, so the display presents an idealized version of mid-twentieth-century America. It's still in the family, and decades-old traditions carry on, most notably a pageant that occurs every half hour, when nightfall descends and houses light up on the display, patriotic and religious slides gleam on the wall, and a recording of Kate Smith belts out "God Bless America."

◆ ◆ ◆

Many tourist areas started by drawing people to a natural wonder. Services and attractions followed, and today many visitors are unaware of the original reason for the area's popularity. Branson, Missouri, was a small town drawing tourists to boat, fish, and browse crafts. A few country music venues entertained as well, but the 1981 movie *Urban Cowboy* triggered an influx of theaters and national performers. A decade later, a *60 Minutes* report on its growth spurred further development. Today some fifty live theaters, featuring some of country music's most popular stars, bring more than seven million visitors per year. Other massive attractions continue to open, such as the new Titanic Museum, shaped like the ocean liner astride an iceberg; Branson Landing shopping district, with a pyrotechnics fountain; and the planned Pinnacle Peak entertainment complex, with a European theme.

The natural attraction that first drew tourists to Branson is the Ozarks, a 33,000-square-mile area across southern Missouri, northwest Arkansas, and northeastern Oklahoma. Although hilly, the region is actually a plateau cut by deep valleys and caves. Damming of the Osage and White Rivers created recreational lakes that have made tourism the leading industry. Branson's Oldtown features shops in the original town center. The pulsing music theaters line MO Route 76, and like other such resorts these days, it now has a Ripley's, Dixie Stampede, IMAX, and other entertainment chains,

but the region's two best-known attractions are west of this more recent development.

The Shepherd of the Hills Homestead tells the story behind Harold Bell Wright's 1907 novel about a family's struggles in the Ozarks and a stranger who comes to be called the "shepherd." A number of buildings recount the story of the people who inspired the author, and performances are presented.

About a mile west of the homestead is Silver Dollar City, a mixture of amusement rides and frontier village. Opened in 1960, it was an outgrowth of adjacent Marvel Cave. To draw more visitors, owner Mary Herschend and her sons, Peter and Jack, rebuilt the mining town near the cave's entrance. The brothers still own the park, but it's grown tremendously. You can enjoy a steam train, music shows, water rides, crafts, a funhouse, and Geyser Gulch, the world's largest treehouse, where all ages can explore rope bridges, towers, windmills, and water guns. The family ran another Silver Dollar City in Pigeon Forge, Tennessee. When country music star Dolly Parton became a partner in 1986, it was renamed Dollywood. In 2003, the family bought the nearby Branson USA and rethemed it as Celebration City, an evenings-only amusement park featuring such Americana as a beachside boardwalk and Route 66–themed rides, restaurants, and golf course.

Two other attractions in the region are Exotic Animal Paradise, with 3,000 animals along a nine-mile driving course, and the Passion Play Complex at Eureka Springs, where the story of Jesus Christ is acted out nightly. The more famous draw here is the seven-story-tall Christ of the Ozarks statue, built in the 1960s, with arms stretching out sixty-five feet.

Some 550 miles to the east is another tourist mecca, sprouted from scenic tourism roots and now grown to megadestination. Great Smoky Mountains National Park covers more than half a million acres, or 800 square miles, almost evenly split between Tennessee and North Carolina. It is by far the most visited of the country's fifty-seven national parks, with more than nine million visi-

My sister and I grew up visiting Paul Bunyan and Babe the Blue Ox in Minnesota. Every northern family trip to visit grandparents included an excursion to Bemidji, with a brief "Get under Babe and smile!" before going back home. I knew that whenever we'd see Grandma and Grandpa, we'd see Paul and Babe, too.

Erika Nelson passes on the tradition to a new generation with her traveling roadside attraction.

Erika Nelson and her big sister Sonja made yearly visits with the family to Bemidji, Minnesota, and took yearly photos, this one from 1984. In 2006, they returned for their grandmother's funeral. "Big family, twenty in my generation, and we all trekked over family by family to stand under Paul and Babe after the service." ERIKA NELSON

When we moved from Texas to Missouri, I remember looking up from a nap in the back of our green AMC Gremlin and seeing a giant eight ball out the window. I asked where we were. "Almost home, honey." From then on, I thought that every town had a giant "thing" so you'd know when you were close to home. We lived near the eight ball and Grandma and Grandpa were by Paul and Babe. It wasn't until much later that I found out the truth.

—ERIKA NELSON, creator and curator of the World's Largest Collection of the World's Smallest Versions of the World's Largest Things Traveling Roadside Attraction and Museum

tors in 2005. (The Grand Canyon had less than half that number, and even fewer visited Yosemite, Olympic, and Yellowstone.) It gets its name from the smokelike fog that hangs over the mountains, produced by rainwater evaporating from the trees. Nearly eighty historic structures from houses to gristmills have been preserved, and about 1,600 black bears live there. Besides numerous campsites, the only lodging is at LeConte Lodge—the only way to reach it is by one of five hiking trails, most of which take about five hours each way. In contrast, you'll find no end to amusements outside the main gates at Gatlinburg, Tennessee. Growth has pushed westward from Gatlinburg to Pigeon Forge and Sevierville. The farther north you go, the more you see modern sprawl.

Those heading to Gatlinburg from the East Coast make a winding but beautiful drive west of Asheville, North Carolina, through Maggie Valley. Overhanging the side of a mountain is the Soco Craft and Tower, with an old-fashioned gift shop. It's hard to resist the small fee to climb the tower for "The Most Photographed View of the Smokeys." Ghost Town in the Sky amusement park can be seen on a distant ridge. Closed since 2002, it reopened in May 2007. The tower attraction was for sale in 2007—business, 1950 building, and nearly five acres for $799,000.

A string of closed motels indicates you're approaching Cherokee. The previous generation's take on the Native American population is in shambles, with names like Papoose and Chief Motels,

New attractions like Ripley's have become a main draw in Gatlinburg, Tennessee.

Reaching Gatlinburg requires a drive over the Smokies, and the only road is straight through the national park. Just before the start of this twisting, stunning drive are a few last nods to the twentieth-century roadside. Of note is the sign for the Pink Motel. As you exit the other side, a commercial bonanza awaits. The area was undeveloped even into the 1920s, but the dedication of the national park in 1940 changed everything. Within a year, a million cars were visiting, and entrepreneurs filled the roads, though the mile-long U.S. 441 through town is hemmed in by the tight size of the Little Pigeon River gorge. This has discouraged full-scale expansion, but chains are here too, notably Ripley's. Gatlinburg's Space

although the Pocahontas Motel remains open to positive reviews. About a mile south of town, just off U.S. 441 (on a stretch of old 441), lies Mac's Indian Village. The 1934 motel has a beautiful but fading neon sign and sixteen cabins fronted by metal half-tepees painted red and outlined in neon. But like so many others here, it closed late in 2005.

Most likely, the motels were done in by the new fifteen-story Harrah's, with its 3,500-video-slot casino. Cherokee is working to move away from stereotypes and develop its Native American heritage. The earliest efforts date to 1950, when the Cherokee Historical Association founded Unto These Hills, a live outdoor pageant where 130 actors and dancers recall the tribe's history. Two years later, the same nonprofit group built the Oconaluftee Indian Village, which re-creates an eighteenth-century settlement. East of town remains at least one roadside attraction from the recent past—Santa's Land Park and Zoo.

The Pink Motel, on the eastern side of the Smokies in Cherokee, North Carolina, sports a stunning sign.

Needle, which opened in 1970, offers a 342-foot-high lookout, but in a sign of changing times, a video arcade has been added at its base. Only a few vintage motels remain among the dozens in Gatlinburg and Pigeon Forge. In keeping with a rustic theme, barbecue restaurants are around every turn. Look for a giant pair of cowboy boots outside Bennett's Pit Bar-B-Que.

About five miles to the north, Pigeon Forge is lined with newer chains and Dollywood. The park has been through various incarnations as Rebel Railroad, Goldrush Junction, and Silver Dollar City before getting its current name in 1986. Dollywood owns the Dixie Stampede, just to the north in Sevierville, where audiences of more than 1,000 watch horseback shows with riders who sing and do tricks, culminating in a battle between North and South. Chicken, ribs, and soup are served home-style—that is, without silverware.

Bears in cages were longtime staples of tourist areas, especially the Smokies, but changing tastes have brought an end to most displays. Regardless, the Three Bears Gift Shop in Pigeon Forge brings in customers, featuring not three but five bears. The animals don't do much, yet tourists can't get enough of them. The souvenir-stuffed store even has plans to rebuild and expand in the next few years.

Such resort areas are often criticized for looking tawdry or tacky, but that's the point. They're not trying to be ritzy. They're supposed to be

Loony Bin in Wisconsin Dells lives up to its name in sheer lunacy.

touristy. You want a place that sells rubber magnets and elongated pennies? You'll find both at Wisconsin Dells, another area created around natural beauty—this one the glacially formed gorge, or dells, of the Wisconsin River, lined with stunning sandstone rock formations. Despite its northern location, the town fifty miles northwest of Madison has morphed into the self-proclaimed "water park capital of the world."

Tourism at Wisconsin Dells grew slowly, focusing on sightseeing. Wisconsin Ducks was started in 1946 to offer tours of the dells in decommissioned amphibious vehicles, or DUKWs, which comes from their military designation—D for 1942, U for utility, K for all-wheel drive, and W for two powered rear axles. In 1952, Tommy Bartlett's traveling water-ski show proved so successful that Bartlett settled the show here permanently. Motels followed, and the area remained a small-scale resort until the water-park bonanza began. The area now offers more than 80 restaurants, 90 attractions, 100 retail shops, and 140 hotels.

Noah's Ark, opened in 1979, has grown to become the country's largest water park. It has dozens of slides and other water thrills, including Time Warp, the "world's largest bowl ride," and Black Anaconda, "America's longest watercoaster," plus a mini-golf, bumper boats, and arcades. The Kalahari Resort claims to be America's largest

Duck boats take tourists to see the original attraction of the Wisconsin Dells.

indoor water park, with a stand-up-and-surf ride and an uphill rollercoaster-type water slide. A merger of three attractions resulted in the Mt. Olympus Water and Theme Park, offering an indoor and outdoor water park, rollercoasters, nine multilevel go-cart tracks, and an indoor theme park. Like many of the mega-attractions, it includes a mini-golf, but visitors can also try Pirate's Cove Adventure Golf, with five eighteen-hole courses that wind around seventeen water-falls and 30,000 plants.

The Tommy Bartlett shows have expanded into the Tommy Bartlett Exploratory, with more than 150 interactive exhibits, such as robots and magic. You also can walk through a forty-three-foot-long Russian Space Station Mir module, one of only three built. At the Loony Bin, a crazy doctor has you search the halls for his monkey by tracking its "monkey poo." Other attractions include Extreme World, with thrill rides and the Castle of Terror. The Haunted Mansion has nine "dreary dungeons of dreadful decor," and the Museum of Historic Torture Devices is sure to enliven your day with such tools of torture as thumbscrews, the rack, and the Chinese death cage.

Less intense adventures awaited at the Wonder Spot, but the "laws of nature gone awry" at this 1952 mystery hill were no match for a road widening after the 2006 season. Nearby Timba-vati Wildlife Park joined with Storybook Gardens in 2004. The wildlife park features interactive shows and even camel rides. The storybook park, which opened in 1956, features fairy-tale scenes with live characters. Like many parks from this era, however, it has to keep up with its new, well-funded, and widely advertised neighbors.

Most resort areas struggle with the conun-drum of keeping older places that regulars love versus encouraging new attractions that bring new customers and higher revenues. Lake George, New York, still has numerous old-style attractions, such as Magic Forest amusement park, but every year progress brings more franchises. The White Mountains in New Hampshire have been able to hold on to a few vintage attractions. Clark's Trad-ing Post in North Woodstock features a bear show

three times a day. Trainer Murray Clark began the operation more than sixty years ago. A two-and-a-half-mile, forty-year-old railroad loop features one of only three wood-burning steam Climax Loco-motives still running and crosses the only stand-ing Howe-Truss covered bridge still in use. And as the workers warn, "Watch out for the wolfman!" Nearby Six Gun City offers rides, miniature horse petting and shows, more than 100 horse-drawn vehicles, and Wild West shows. James and Eleanor Brady and their eight children built it on their farm and opened it in 1957. With three genera-tions now involved, the family says it's still driven by the original plan "to be an affordable place where families of all sizes can leave their troubles behind and enjoy a day of entertainment based on a time long since gone by."

Both the Atlantic and Pacific Coasts are full of towns that can be considered destinations. After years of low-key development because of short summer seasons, commercial growth has arrived at many of these resorts. The Wildwoods in New Jersey responded in 1997 with the Doo Wop Preservation League to save and promote the abundance of ebullient mid-1950s businesses in their three coastal towns. Though condomini-ums have nudged out some classic motels, the increased awareness has led to restorations of

The entrance to the Tommy Bartlett Exploratory in Wisconsin Dells is through a re-created space capsule.

The rooms, pool, and plastic palm trees glow each evening at the Caribbean Motel in Wildwood Crest, New Jersey. KYLE WEAVER

James' Salt Water Taffy lights up the night in Wildwood, New Jersey. KYLE WEAVER

signs and buildings. One of the most notable is the 1956 Caribbean Motel. With design elements like a levitating ramp, crescent-shaped pool, and plastic palm trees, its style could be called tropical futurism. Some of the chains, such as Subway, Commerce Bank, and Harley-Davidson have joined in the fun and now feature new buildings and signs designed in Doo Wop style.

At Point Pleasant Beach, New Jersey, Jenkinson's Boardwalk is a traditional seaside park geared toward children. Founded in 1927, it offers the perfect combo, with rides, arcades, mini-golf, an aquarium, and snacks, all on a manageable, not overly commercialized scale. It also has a funhouse, little bumper cars, a small coaster, and the famed spinning Super Himalaya ride. Jenkinson's Sweet Shop is open year-round.

In Myrtle Beach, South Carolina, preservation is a challenge, with fourteen million visitors to the area every year. It's a popular golf resort and the largest community in the "Grand Strand," which stretches from Georgetown to Little River. The town has been a big tourist draw since the 1970s, and recent years have brought condos and

The sign for the Gay Dolphin, family-owned since the 1940s, towers above a new Ripley's attraction in Myrtle Beach, South Carolina.

other large-scale development. Although Family Kingdom Amusement Park survives, the loss of the Pavilion Park after the 2006 season was especially hard for many Myrtle Beach residents and regular visitors. One local penned the song, "Why Do You Want to Tear the Pavilion Down?" Not far away, a more modern amusement park is under way: Hard Rock Park, based on the restaurant chain, is being built on the site of the former Waccamaw Factory Shoppes. Park areas and attractions will have a rock music theme.

A few resort areas retain their mid-twentieth century ambience. Geneva-on-the-Lake in Ohio, has been compared to Mayberry, the fictional town in *The Andy Griffith Show*, because it's small enough that most of the residents know each other. Many of its businesses have been around since the 1950s. There are no chain motels and restaurants here, though they may not be too far off. In 2004, a conference center and hotel opened at the adjacent Geneva State Park. At the close of the 2006 season, Erieview kiddie park was closed and the rides auctioned off. Owner Donald "Woody" Woodward said the crowds were there and he enjoyed

Time Square next to the entry to Erieview Park, Geneva-on-the-Lake.

the business, but his income was being outpaced by skyrocketing insurance, workers' compensation, and even ride licenses. He plans on using the 700-foot property as a lakefront boardwalk.

While strolling the few blocks lined with vintage arcades and ice cream stands, stop by tiny Madsen Donuts, still using the same recipes since 1938. Or you can take a side street toward the lake to Mary's Kitchen, a cozy restaurant in a house. Other food treasures await too. Perhaps the most classic hangout is Eddie's Grill, with a sparkling outdoor counter that glows under yellow bulbs at night, orange benches lining the sidewalk, and enclosed El Patio dining area with tabletop Seeburg jukebox Wall-O-Matics and matching speakers. Eddie Sezon opened the stand in 1949 when he was seventeen, and little has changed since then. You can still get a foot-long hot dog or a Slovenian sausage sandwich and root beer served from countertop barrels. At the Sandy Chanty, the emphasis is on seafood, from breaded alligator to Lobster Crawl Lasagna. The walls and tables sport nautical touches, but the best surprise is behind the bar: an old-time shooting gallery! Owner Patt Bowen found it when she went looking for storage space one day. Old-timers remembered it. They heard that it was first used at Coney Island in 1928, then installed here in 1937,

The shooting gallery at the Sandy Chanty in Geneva-on-the-Lake.

but covered in 1980. Patt will turn it on briefly if you ask, and the targets will spin and clank as they did in the days when customers took shots at them.

Another town, much larger, also retains a great many vintage businesses. Manitou Springs grew along with the gold mines discovered in the late 1850s around Pikes Peak, seventy miles south of Denver and just west of Colorado Springs. When the gold ran out, locals turned to the mineral-rich, bubbling springs, long used by Native Americans for their curative waters. An old stagecoach inn was redeveloped as the Cliff House and became the place to stay for wealthy visitors. It prospered into the twentieth century, and the town's numerous surviving midcentury motels embody those times. By 1981, as the rich looked farther afield for tony retreats, the Cliff House was converted to apartments. A fire the next year nearly destroyed it, and the building sat abandoned until 1997, when it was restored and refurbished.

Classic roadside attractions in the area include Santa's Workshop and Garden of the Gods Trading Post, both discussed later in this book. Among the natural attractions at Manitou Springs are the Manitou Cliff Dwellings, Garden of the Gods rock formations, Cave of the Winds, and Pikes Peak, towering 14,110 feet. In 1806, when Zebulon Pike tried, but failed, to reach the top, he predicted that no one else would ever make it up

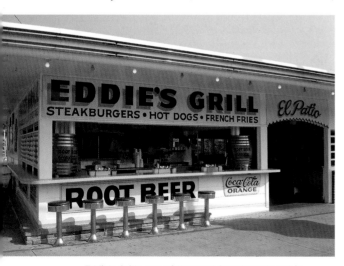

Eddie's Grille, one of the most fun places to eat in Geneva-on-the-Lake.

The elegant Cliff House overlooks the arcade in Manitou Springs, Colorado, but at left, the Manitou Spa, built in 1920, now sits closed. Plans call for renovating it into loft apartments.

either. By 1889, a carriage road was carved to the top, and two years later, it could be reached by a cog railway, named for a middle gearlike wheel to help on steep grades. Pikes Peak Cog Railway remains the world's highest cog railroad and the highest train in the United States. In 1893, Katharine Lee Bates was so inspired by her wagon ride up the peak that she penned "America the Beautiful."

Most of the motels, shops, and restaurants in Manitou Springs line Manitou Avenue. The El Colorado Lodge, built in 1926, features adobe cabins with pine ceiling beams and wood-burning fireplaces. Town-N-Country Cottages, also with adobe-style rooms, is a few blocks above town in a rural setting. The Best Value Inn Villa Motel retains a few cinderblock duplex cabins along the main street, hidden behind trees. At the Timber Lodge, cabins built in the 1930s through 1950s are set among trees and a stream.

An arcade in the middle of Manitou Springs has an astounding assortment of games from the past, from mechanical basketball, hockey, football, and 1950s pinball machines to Ms. Pac Man

The surviving welcome arch in Manitou Springs and the Mel-Haven, just one of dozens of vintage motels in the area.

and Donkey Kong. There's even a Relax-A-Lator for tired feet. More than 250 games are spread among buildings that echo with retro videogame sounds and laughter.

SPOTLIGHT ON
Mini-Golf

The first mini-golf, a private course, was built in 1918, but the first one open to the public is widely reported to have been Tom Thumb Golf, created in 1926 by Garnet and Frieda Carter, atop Lookout Mountain, where they later developed the famous Rock City. Early courses emphasized landscaping, with stonework, ponds, and floral arrangements. Playing surfaces were turf or sand, and side rails were made of wood.

East Potomac Golf Course in Washington, D.C., claims to have opened in 1921, but that's only true of the neighboring full-size course. The small one, once called Circus Mini Golf Putt-4-Fun, opened in 1930. The honor of oldest course still operating probably goes to Allison's Mini Golf in Geneva-on-the-Lake, Ohio. A sign there proclaims that it's America's oldest continually operated course, since 1924, though we haven't received confirmation on this. Obstacles include dangling bowling pins, a bumper-filled bridge crossing, and a classic metal loop-the-loop. The Allison family has owned the course since 1981. Putts 'N Prizes, in Lake George, New York, also says it's the oldest, but it dates to 1929.

The sport was further popularized in the 1940s by brothers Robert and Joseph Taylor, who created elaborate obstacles and custom-designed courses. They built their first one in Williamsport, Pennsylvania, and then spread their handiwork to New York State. Their holes were formed to include windmills, lighthouses, wishing wells, and pinball machines. The military even had them prefabricate courses for use in Asia and Africa.

By the 1950s, green carpet was being used to top the course surface, imitating grass. Just outside Cleveland, Ohio, the Memphis Championship Miniature Golf Course features classic obstacles and decorations of the era, such as a Ferris wheel and lighthouse. It's part of the Memphis Kiddie Park, opened in 1952, which also has eleven miniature rides.

In Gatlinburg, Tennessee, classic courses like Jolly Golf and Bunny Golf have closed, but hanging in there, literally on a hillside, is Hillbilly Golf. An incline takes players 300 feet uphill to a pair of eighteen-hole downward-descending courses, both lined with cliché backwoods symbols, such as stills and outhouses. Newer attractions such as Ripley's Davy Crockett Mini Golf feature interactive holes, with well-placed shots making gophers sing or cannons fire.

One of the most elaborate courses is Par-King, just north of Chicago. Since opening in the 1960s, it has been called the Taj Mahal of mini-golfs. It includes big wooden carousel horses, water obstacles, mechanical objects, and even a 750-piece roller coaster.

The big shift toward today's over-the-top architecture began at Jungle Golf in Myrtle Beach, South Carolina. A mountain with waterfalls flowing into a pond dominated the course, which reduced play to tackling hills and curves. As fiberglass became common in the 1950s and 1960s, it was used to build giant figures on the courses, often to follow a theme, such as animals or fairy tales. A nightmare inspired Goofy Golf owner Lee Koplin to add monsters and other scary creatures to his course. The combination of catchy novelty and easy-to-maintain (and play) holes was quickly and widely imitated. Myrtle Beach itself has become the self-proclaimed mini-golf capital of the world.

The oldest survivor there may be Rainbow Falls Golf from the 1960s, but today gargantuan modern courses line the long main drag from Myrtle Beach to North

Allison's Mini Golf in Geneva-on-the-Lake is the country's oldest continuously operated course.

Myrtle Beach. At Mount Atlanticus Minotaur Goff (yes, goff), next to where Pavilion Amusement Park once stood, the operators tell the story that the course broke away from Atlantis 50,000 years ago and washed up at Myrtle Beach in 1998 atop Chapin's department store. The tropical-archaeological-fantasy-themed attraction, on top of a three-story Art Deco building, has been named best mini-golf course in the world by the Miniature Golf Association and the International Recreational Go-Kart Association. The nearby Mayday Mini Golf is dominated by a crashed plane and rescue helicopter hovering over the course. Other new ones, many with a nautical or tiki theme, include Captain Hook's, Spyglass, Lost Treasure, Jurassic, Dragon's Lair, Shipwreck Island, and NASCAR Challenge. Hawaiian Rumble, whose owners also run Hawaiian Caverns and Hawaiian Village, is perhaps the most famous, rated the best course by *Golf* magazine. It serves as the headquarters of the U.S. Professional

Hillbilly Golf in Gatlinburg, Tennessee, has a little incline that takes players to the top of the course.

FAN FAVORITE

Even though I'd been conditioned by thousands of miles of roadside rambles, documenting the odd and unique icons of the American byways, my first encounter with Goofy Golf, along the Gulf Highway in Biloxi, Mississippi, was exceptional.

It was 1983 and we were on our way to a friend's wedding in New Orleans. Suddenly, looming up amid the fast-food franchises and mini-marts, was a giant moving skull. We stopped at the course for an eighteen-hole round. Here were the classics, assembled in a hallucinogenic array of cross-cultural references—a big Buddha, a huge Sphinx, dancing monkeys, chomping red-eyed alligators, descending spiders, colorful dinosaurs, anthropomorphic trees, giant ants, rocket ships, trolls, and a final walk into an enormous conch shell.

We returned a few days later, and I made a short video documentary on this roadside gem, one of several courses constructed by Lee Koplin out of Panama City, Florida.

In 2001, we returned to New Orleans and made a coastal detour to revisit our favorite mini-golf. Sadly, we found that Goofy Golf had been turned into a parking lot for a pirate-themed gambling casino.

—KEN BROWN, filmmaker, photographer, cartoonist, and postcard publisher of pop culture and roadside vernacular

The Biloxi Goofy Golf in Mississippi in 1983, since demolished. KEN BROWN

FAN FAVORITE

What became known as the "dinosaur and windmill" style of miniature golf course originated with the Goofy Golf chain founded by Lee Koplin. Reportedly, Koplin built his first concrete figures for a course in Guerneville, California, but his idea really made a hole in one when he began building his string of fantasy-lands along the Southeast's Gulf Coast in the late 1950s. Courses in Biloxi, Mississippi, and Pensacola and Fort Walton Beach, Florida, preceded his 1959 masterpiece in Panama City Beach, also in Florida.

I first saw this collection of prehistoric animals and archaeological landmarks in 1968 at age five, and I could not figure out what the place was supposed to be. It was not until two years later that my parents decided I was old enough to learn how to play mini-golf. I never did get to be very good at the game, but I sure spent a lot of time photographing the statuary, which came in handy for future research.

Goofy Golf survives as one of the only examples of vintage tourism along the rapidly overdeveloping Panama City Beach strip. Even its neighbor, the classic Miracle Strip Amusement Park, turned off its lights for the last time on Labor Day 2004 to make way for yet another condo complex. Who knows how long Goofy Golf will be able to stand its ground as expensive, high-rise condominiums devour the property surrounding it?

—TIM HOLLIS, author, *Dixie Before Disney*; *Glass Bottom Boats & Mermaid Tails: Florida's Tourist Springs*; *Florida's Miracle Strip: From Redneck Riviera to Emerald Coast*; and *The Land of the Smokies: Great Mountain Memories*

Goofy Golf, the lone reminder in Panama City, Florida, of its vibrant twentieth-century heyday. TIM HOLLIS

Mini Golf Association, with a members-only training center. In the middle of all the action, a forty-foot-tall volcano erupts every twenty minutes.

But don't think mom-and-pop ingenuity are a thing of the past. Artist and author Maria Reidelbach built the Gnome on the Range Mini-Golf, landscaped with fruits, vegetables, and herbs, as part of The Fun Farm attrac-tion in New York State. She already had experience (with help from Ken Brown and hundreds of volunteers) reno-vating and redesigning a run-down miniature golf course in New York City's Hudson River Park into Goofy Garden Golf. Next up for the farm is the world's largest corn cow, thirty-feet tall and covered in the equivalent amount of food that a cow consumes to grow to maturity.

CHAPTER 2

ROUTE 66
THE 2,448-MILE ATTRACTION

Route 66 enjoys a level of celebrity like no other road. Since the dawn of limited-access highways, two-lane roads have been romanticized and mythologized, but Route 66 surpasses them all. Its history, its iconic sites, and even its name have garnered worldwide attention. The mystique that has grown up around Route 66 has rendered it a symbol for adventure, and for America itself.

The origins of 66, and the fortuitous choice of its alliterative number, is an entertaining saga. As the federal highway system was being developed in the mid-1920s, there was no single route from Chicago to Los Angeles. Drivers took a combination of wagon paths and auto trails. The plan for numbering highways assigned even numerals to east-west routes, with multiples of ten for the most important transcontinentals, such as U.S. 30 or U.S. 40. The road was not nearly coast to coast and crossed Illinois and Missouri on a diagonal, but the anticipated volume of traffic led to its being designated U.S. 60 late in 1925. The plan began to unravel when Kentucky complained that it was not going to get a multiple of ten, and it wanted part of 60. Rather than break up their

Juan Delgadillo, founder of the Snow Cap Drive-In along Old Route 66 in Seligman, Arizona, has passed away, but his beloved crazy antics live on. Here son John offers up a wad of dirty napkins as part of his schtick. The young customer who ordered a small cone got a *very* small one.

Chicago–to–Los Angeles route into different numbers, proponents of a single numeral, led by Cyrus Avery, chairman of the Oklahoma Highway Commission and member of the federal numbering committee, chose U.S. 66 on April 30, 1926. U.S. 60 ended up less than transcontinental, connecting Virginia Beach to Springfield, Missouri, indeed crossing the length of Kentucky.

Route 66 took travelers from Lake Michigan through Missouri and Oklahoma before entering the empty, enchanting landscape of the Southwest. As Arthur Krim has written in *Route 66: Iconography of the American Highway*, "The unique numbers gave U.S. Highway 66 an appealing identity as a road of scenic wonders through New Mexico and Arizona before the Great Depression and the Dust Bowl migration reset the sixes as signs of exodus to California." This migration was famously recounted by John Steinbeck in *The Grapes of Wrath*, his 1939 novel about the Joad family and other "Okies" struggling to reach California. Route 66 came to embody the American tradition of starting over by heading west—an adventure for some, the last chance for others.

In early 1946, Bobby Troup penned his ode to Route 66 as he and his wife made their way from Pennsylvania to Hollywood. Troupe's eastern accent showed in his pronunciation of "route" as "root" and not "rout," as said along the high-

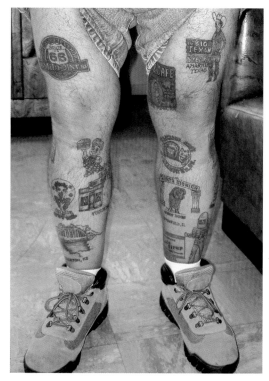

**Fans like Ron Jones are compelled to express their devotion to Route 66.
Jones shows his ink at the Mid Point Café in Adrian, Texas.**

Trading posts are my favorite memories of traveling with my family on vacation way back when. I bet Dad got tired of me and my brother trying to get him to stop at every one we saw along the highway. Those colorful outposts always had a wealth of treas-

Guy Randall with his mom, Pat, and brother Gary on their family vacation along Route 66 in 1956. Dad Howard snapped the pic. GUY RANDALL

ures to enchant young kids like us. Souvenir postcards of jackalopes, packages of rattlesnake eggs, cactus candy, tumbled stones, and "Indian" goods from Japan made it hard to choose what to buy. My brother and I were enchanted with the plastic tomahawks, colorful dyed-feather headdresses, and cardboard-and-rubber tom-toms. Once we talked our parents into buying a tom-tom at one of those old trading posts. My brother and I pounded out rhythmic beats in time to the *thump-thump* of tires on the old highway we traveled down. It wasn't long before our parents regretted their decision. A day or so into our trip, the tom-tom developed a mysterious cut, rendering it useless.

Once, outside Gallup, New Mexico, on Old Route 66, my mom spied an old Native American woman along the highway displaying her ceramic wares. Mom traded some homemade fudge for a couple pieces of pottery. I still have one of those wonderful pots, a prized memento of our family vacation through the Southwest fifty years ago.

—GUY RANDALL, The Road Wanderer, www.theroadwanderer.net

way itself. The song was recorded within a month of his arrival by the King Cole Trio, who provided a jazzy beat to the twelve-bar blues. GIs returning from World War II and Korea followed the lyrics west on family vacations or in search of work.

The establishment of the interstate highway system in 1956 began a piecemeal replacement of federal routes by four-lane freeways. The 1960s TV series *Route 66*, with characters Tom and Buzz cruising the highway in a Corvette, again fueled the public's imagination, but by the late 1970s, interstates had superseded most two-lanes. In 1984, the completion of a bypass around Williams, Arizona, marked the final replacement of Route 66. The next year, U.S. 66 was decommissioned. Highway shields came down, and the number was erased from maps.

Although the interstates brought decline, it was this very descent that became fascinating, even fashionable. Fans and academics launched

The Painted Desert Trading Post is on a long-abandoned stretch of Route 66 in eastern Arizona.

interest groups and historical surveys to celebrate and document the road. One of the leaders of this movement was Angel Delgadillo, a barber in Seligman, Arizona, who helped form the Historic Route 66 Association of Arizona in 1987. Towns renamed their streets Historic Route 66 and mounted publicity campaigns to pull drivers off the interstates. Congress even passed an act in 1999 that created the Route 66 Corridor Preservation Program, administered through the National Park Service, to help individuals and organizations address preservation needs. Books, travel articles, and a line of clothing reignited the allure and imbued the road with an aura of fun and excitement, danger and escape, nostalgia and melancholy—sometimes real, often imagined.

◆ ◆ ◆

We set out on our 66 odyssey with no particular plan. We'd collected postcards for years and had driven part of the route in Illinois, but we'd never made the big trip; a drive to the West Coast and back requires a fair amount of time.

If you want to follow the highway, just drive the old two-lane between towns along the route, which is how we began. We were spoiled by starting in Illinois, where the National Scenic Byways Program has marked the route very well. The road in New Mexico and Arizona is also well designated, and most states have some sort of signage. Sometimes, though, we'd get far enough off track that we knew we'd missed a sign. As we were later told, the missing signs were likely taken as souvenirs. To counter theft, state and local enthusiast groups increasingly paint the 66 shield on the pavement.

Also helpful are the free guides found along the way; just about every state offers a map and directory of attractions. Lots of books have been written about the road. In Afton, Oklahoma, we met longtime roadsider Laurel Kane in her beautifully restored D-X gas station and picked up Jerry McClanahan's *EZ66 Guide*. It's fun, informative, and a fabulous aid for learning where the road goes and what's along it. Here are some other guides:

FAN FAVORITE

There's definitely no shortage of wacky roadside Americana along what's left of Route 66, but the most endearing of them all has to be Tinkertown. Created over the past sixty-odd years by Ross and Carla Ward and family, Tinkertown is an old-fashioned penny arcade run riot, housed in a ramshackle building made in part out of glass bottles and bicycle wheels, tucked away in the pine-forested mountains of New Mexico. Among the many odds and ends, one display case holds over 100-plus plastic figures from the tops of wedding cakes. More than a thousand delicately carved miniature wooden figures are featured in animated scenes, such as a circus big top complete with sideshow and a Wild West town with dance-hall girls and a squawking vulture. The spirit of the place is aptly summed up by the Tinkertown motto, "We did all this while you were watching TV."

—JAMIE JENSEN, author of *Road Trip USA*, www.roadtripusa.com

One of the many carved scenes at Tinkertown, near Albuquerque.

- AAA's *Greatest Hits* laminated fold-out map points out the most famous attractions for beginners.

- The National Historic Route 66 Federation's slim *Dining & Lodging Guide* lists more than 400 places, with price ranges, specialties, and phone numbers.

- Drew Knowles's *Adventure Handbook*, now in a greatly expanded third edition, does not give directions but provides the history behind most every town and roadside diversion. Lots of photos and recommended side trips make it enjoyable for the armchair traveler and helpful to those on the road.

- The best value is Emily Priddy's guide for kids, available for free download at www.kidson66.com, which we found suits adults just fine. Major and lesser-known attractions are described, along with basic information for visiting.

There are other good guides too, but these are the ones that helped us.

Two things struck us most from this trip. One is that we imagined Route 66 to always be far from civilization, but in general it isn't. There are long stretches between towns, and some desert sections are startling in their isolation, but the interstates that bypassed the old road are never far, sometimes only a few feet away. We envisioned the U-Drop Inn at a lonely crossroads, but it is actually at a street corner in Shamrock, a small but nonetheless active town.

The other interesting thing is the sense of community along the corridor. Unlike any other road we've traveled, we could tell we were on Route 66 by the camaraderie among proprietors, town boosters, and tourists, no matter the state. It also was fun to keep bumping into folks who were likewise touring the road from east to

By the mid-1990s, the 66 Drive-In Theater in Carthage, Missouri, was closed and decrepit. Cars and parts from a salvage business littered the lot, and weeds had grown into trees, but a miraculous restoration led to its reopening in 1998.

The Lost Snake Pit entered my family's mythology in the 1960s. Dad hated to stop on our breakneck journeys along Route 66, so the one time we paused to see the rattlers at a trading post should be a cherished recollection, except I was just too young to remember.

All I know is that this ratty reptile resort was in New Mexico or Arizona—a white building festooned with signs. Mom locked herself in the car while Dad led me inside, only to leave in a huff. It seems the snakes were dead and we had wasted a precious stop. The identity of the Lost Snake Pit remains a mystery.

—JERRY MCCLANAHAN, artist and author of *EZ66 Guide for Travelers*

west. An early morning stop at Ted Drewes' Frozen Custard found us meeting lots of fellow fans, including Yvonne and Richard from the Netherlands, taking a month to tour the road. Every few hours or days, we'd cross paths and compare notes.

Above: The Eisler Brothers Old Riverton Store in Riverton, Kansas, has been selling groceries since 1925. The tiny, tin-ceiling store also has a gift shop.

Left, middle: At her restored 1930s gas station (canopy outside and tin ceiling inside) in Afton, Oklahoma, Laurel Kane displays Route 66 memorabilia, particularly from one of her favorite places, the Buffalo Ranch, recently demolished to make way for a convenience store. Her ex-husband's vintage Packards will be on display in the connected garage after that portion is restored.

Left, bottom: Dawn Welch, owner of the Rock Café in Stroud, Oklahoma, was the inspiration for Sally the Porsche in *Cars*, hence the cool cutouts. Specialties include fried pickles and oatmeal pie. The café was built with stones unearthed when Route 66 was paved.

Below: Kay Farmer, showing her famous French Silk Pie, has operated the Country Dove in Elk City, Oklahoma, with Glenna Hollis since 1983. The staff and customers all seemed to know each other and were very welcoming to tired travelers.

The photos here document some of our most interesting stops, but we also enjoyed the places listed below:

- The Launching Pad Café in Wilmington, Illinois, has great drive-in food and the Gemini Giant, a towering outer-space mascot—actually, a remodeled Muffler Man.

- Chain of Rocks Bridge was worth the bumpy ride to the Mississippi River overlook in Illinois to see it. Two weeks later, we stopped on the Missouri side to walk onto the span.

- Route 66 State Park, west of St. Louis, has a wonderful museum and gift shop housed in a 1935 roadhouse. The park encompasses the former summer resort town of Times Beach along the Meramec River.

- Springfield, Missouri—where we ate an excellent dinner at Cielito Lindo and a very creamy dessert at Andy's Frozen Custard—was enjoyable. We retired to a classic motel at the Rail Haven. Photo collages in each room detailed the history from 1938, including its early joining with Best Western. In the retro lobby, we

Like the better-known Cadillac Ranch near Amarillo, Texas, the Bug Ranch in Conway, nineteen miles east of the city, features classic cars nose-down in the ground. The Volkswagen Beetles were installed by the Crutchfield family, owners of the adjacent Longhorn Trading Post, which was closed when we recently visited.

Among the many dazzling vintage stations along Route 66, perhaps the best known is the Tower Station and U-Drop-Inn of Shamrock, Texas. This Art Deco beauty was built in 1936 and renovated in 2003. It now houses a tourist info center and small gift shop.

Eat a seventy-two-ounce steak in one hour at the Big Texan in Amarillo, Texas, and it's free. Otherwise, you fork over $72. (Actually, it's pay before you eat, just in case.) The business started in 1960 along Route 66 (now Amarillo Boulevard) but moved to the newly completed I-40 in 1970. The complex includes a motel with both western and southwestern-style façades and interiors. And, by the way, of the 42,000 who have tried eating the seventy-two-ouncer, only about 7,000 have succeeded.

Tucumcari, New Mexico, is a treasure trove of roadside delights. Mike Callens at Tee Pee Curios recalls when the street was lined with curio shops. His is the last of the old-timers.

bought some repro postcards. We left too early the next morning to try the Steak 'n Shake along St. Louis Street, its 1962 design embodying the vibrancy of classic 1950s-meets-Jetsons. West of town is the former Rock Fountain Court, now Melinda Court, with tidy stone cottages.

- The Blue Whale at Catoosa, Oklahoma, is an oasis of calm and old-time fun along a busy highway. Completed in 1972, it closed in 1988 and declined until 1995, when restoration was begun. The eighty-foot-long whale required 126 bags of concrete mix, 2,400 linear feet of wood, and almost 10 tons of crushed stone.

- McLean, Texas, shows the effects of being bypassed. Though home to the Devil's Rope Museum, it also has a surprising number of abandoned stations, including a beautifully restored Phillips 66 station.

- The Mid-Point Café in Adrian, Texas, features the famous Ugly Crust Pie. While there, we met Joy Avery, the granddaughter of Cyrus Avery, Father of Route 66. The gift shop was a nice surprise too.

- Albuquerque's Central Avenue offers slices of roadside history. We spent a couple hours before the morning rush hour photographing coffee shops, vintage signs, a Valentine diner that is now a police station, a Route 66 welcome arch, and lots of motels, including the endangered El Vado.

- The Frontier Restaurant was recommended by our friend Nick Ciotola, who attended the University of New Mexico in Albuquerque. He suggested we try green sauce, a salsa made from tomatillos that is both sweet and spicy. He was right about the Frontier, but eating the sauce with our meal was a high point of the trip.

Trading Posts like the Teepee line the route at the New Mexico-Arizona border.

Four of the many neon signs that can be found in Gallup, New Mexico.

Ed Galloway's Totem Pole Park in Oklahoma is a highly personal place, which appeals to my taste in roadside attractions. Nathan "Ed" Galloway lived with his wife, Villie, a short distance from Route 66 and spent his later years, beginning in 1937, quietly sculpt-ing a collection of dozens of Native American-inspired structures, the most prominent of which is a ninety-foot-tall totem pole. Most of these creations are fes-tooned with brightly colored reliefs depicting fish, birds, reptiles, and other motifs consistent with Ed's high regard for the culture.

Also on the property is an eleven-sided building Ed constructed to house the expanding collection of fid-dles he was carving. Though most of them have been lost to theft or damage, the fiddle collection is thought to have reached about 300.

I strongly urge you to visit Totem Pole Park, sup-ported by the Rogers County Historical Society, and surround yourself with the evidence of Ed Galloway's prodigious creative energies. He was speaking to you and me when he said, "All my life, I did the best I knew. I built these things by the side of the road to be a friend to you."

—DREW KNOWLES, author of *Route 66 Adventure Handbook*, www.Route66University.com

Totem Pole Park near Foyil, Oklahoma. DREW KNOWLES

- The El Rancho Hotel in Gallup, New Mexico, charms with its old-time style. Opened in 1937, it was the idea of R. E. Griffith, brother of the better-known D. W. Griffith, both film directors. Its western decor was fitting for a place that served as headquarters for numer-ous movies filmed in the area, particularly Westerns, such as *Streets of Laredo*, starring William Holden. Other stars in the register include Kirk Douglas, Spencer Tracy, and Katharine Hepburn.

- Wigwam Village in Arizona features fifteen free-standing rooms, each shaped like a tepee. Inside the concrete cabins are beds, full bath, air conditioning, and color TV, all for about $50 a night.

- The corner that has come to represent *the* "Standin' on a corner in Winslow, Arizona," from the 1972 Eagles song "Take It Easy" is nice, though the nearest building recently burned down and the corner is fenced off. You'll never hear the song again without say-ing you've been on that corner.

- The Route 66 Gift Shop and Museum in Selig-man, Arizona, has loads of books, T-shirts, and other ephemera, matched only by the kindness of the owners. It was closing time when we arrived, but Angel Delgadillo, his wife Vilma, and their son-in-law Mauricio Perez stopped what they were doing to let us shop and snap pictures at their barbershop turned tourist mecca.

- The 73-mile drive west to Kingman is one of the longest stretches away from the interstate, and the little settlements and train racing alongside us at twilight made for a spellbinding trip.

At least a dozen wild burros roam the streets in the isolated town of Oatman, Arizona, sometimes visiting stores like Arizona Girls Candles. They are descendants of a herd turned loose after the gold mines played out around World War II. Though now far off the beaten path, the Oatman Hotel was host to honeymooners Clark Gable and Carole Lombard in 1939.

- The slow drive into the Black Mountains and over Sitgreaves Pass to Oatman is exhilarating; comic, when burros block the way; and terrifying, when you see wrecks below as you creep around the hairpin turns. We were humbled when a shop owner in town said she commutes from Kingman daily.

- The arrangements of rocks into words and images along the lonely desert stretch near Amboy are all the more amazing as they go on mile after mile.

As on all old roads, there are many other places we had to pass by. Places like Funk's Grove, home of pure maple sirup—that's how they spell it to indicate it has no sugar added—where the Funk family has been tapping trees for nearly two centuries. Or the Wigwam Motel in Rialto, California, long run-down but now all spruced up. There's never enough time, but there's always next year.

Few cars pass Roy's Café in Amboy, California, leaving it as only an outpost for bottled water, but on 125-degree days in the Mojave Desert, that's OK.

43

SPOTLIGHT ON
the Lincoln Highway

A third longer than Route 66 and a dozen years older, the Lincoln Highway nonetheless lags when it comes to recognition. Its name was celebrated for decades, surviving in many towns as Lincoln Way, but the curvy 66 shield and its intense promotion have made it hard to compete. Starting in 1913, the founders of the Lincoln Highway mounted a publicity bonanza, marking the route with red, white, and blue stripes painted on telephone poles. The Lincoln continues to represent early motoring—spindly black cars in mud and overnight stays in a field or at a farmhouse—while 66 is associated with Corvettes and postwar prosperity.

The Lincoln's rebirth began in the late 1980s, when Drake Hokanson's evocative *The Lincoln Highway: Main Street Across America* rekindled interest along the coast-to-coast road. Every year, more guides are published, businesses restored, and trips made along the 3,300 miles from New York to San Francisco. People are increasingly drawn to the romance of that earlier time, the slower pace, and the geography and history lessons that unfold as you make your way across the country.

From Times Square in New York City, the route is clogged through urban areas of New Jersey, but taverns and diners show up on the way to Pennsylvania Dutch country. Then it's over the Alleghenies, through Pittsburgh, into the flat farms of Ohio and Indiana, and around the busy suburbs of Chicago. Corn and dairy cows in Iowa and eastern Nebraska turn into wheat and

The Fort Cody Trading Post in North Platte, Nebraska, is the most recent in a long line of souvenir stands run by the Henline family. The store is filled with all sorts of fun things, including a working model of the Buffalo Bill Wild West Show.

beef cattle by Wyoming and the leg that dips down to Denver, Colorado. The highway climbs from Cheyenne into the high plains of the northern Rockies, passes through Salt Lake City, and skirts the Great Salt Desert. Then it crosses the folded basin of Nevada on "the Loneliest Road in America" and heads to the bright lights of Reno. The route has two alternatives around Lake Tahoe—over the infamous Donner Summit or through pine forests to Placerville—and descends into Sacramento. Another splitting of routes rejoins in San Francisco, and the highway makes its way to Lincoln Park overlooking the Pacific. Early motorists dipped their tires in the ocean before departing on cross-country voyages. If they persevered, they did the same in the water on the opposite coast.

The Highway Garage in Livermore, California, was built by Frank Duarte in 1915 and soon expanded to sell Durant, Flint, and Star automobiles. It was to be demolished for a park in the 1970s, when the Livermore Heritage Guild saved and restored the garage. It now also houses a small transportation museum but is open only occasionally.

The Shoe House in York, Pennsylvania, was built by "Shoe Wizard" Mahlon Haines in 1948 as an advertising gimmick for his chain of forty shoe stores. He offered free stays to elderly couples and honeymooners who registered in his stores.

CHAPTER 3

AMUSING PLACES

Coney Island's Cyclone opened on June 26, 1927, and remains one of the most famous and popular roller coasters. Now part of Astroland, the Cyclone sits at the same site as the world's first roller coaster and world's first successful looping coaster.

Who can forget the kiddielands of their youth? The chance to be the driver of a car or the pilot of an airplane or spaceship was exciting. If the rides were from the era of tailfins and big colorful bulbs, chances are they also made a sound you can't shake from your head, an incessant buzzing, whether automatic or produced by a horn button, which you could hear every kid pushing throughout the park.

You might not think of small amusement parks as roadside attractions, but they have all the classic ingredients: small-scale, family-operated, with mid-twentieth-century architecture, porcelain-enamel signs, and vintage neon. They usually offer free admission to the park with pay-as-you-go rides. But few of these parks actually remain. More often, vintage kiddie rides are part of full-scale vintage parks, such as Conneaut Lake Park in western Pennsylvania, opened in 1892 and best known for its Blue Streak coaster. More often, the fate of such parks is similar to the previously mentioned Erieview Park, not far away in Geneva-on-the-Lake, Ohio. It opened as Pera's Kiddy Park in 1945, with two rides. It had since expanded to nine adult and nine junior rides,

Streamlined cars proudly announced their home at Erieview Park, but it closed after the 2006 season.

many vintage, but by the end of the 2006 season, the family had decided to sell the rides and redevelop the land because of skyrocketing costs.

Besides Conneaut, Pennsylvania has many other classic parks, such as Waldameer, overlooking Lake Erie since 1896, and DelGrosso's and Lakemont, near Altoona. Lakemont, opened in 1894, is home to the 1902 Leap the Dips, the world's oldest roller coaster. Idlewild, in Ligonier, added Story Book Forest in 1956 and more recently a trolley ride through Mister Rogers' Neighborhood of Make-Believe. Under the same ownership near Pittsburgh is Kennywood, which bills itself as "America's Favorite Traditional Amusement Park." The 1898 park is becoming more like its larger cousins but retains many classic rides and architectural details, such as a massive 1926 Dentzel carousel with 1916 tiger-oak Wurlitzer band organ, all recently restored. Kennywood also still lets you bring your lunch in a picnic basket if you like. Perhaps the state's most beloved park is Knoebels, with its programmatic architecture, 1973 Haunted Mansion dark ride, and many classic kiddie rides. It's also the largest free admission park in the United States.

New York State, likewise, retains a slew of vintage parks. In the Adirondacks, Enchanted Forest opened July 7, 1956, featuring Storybook Lane Little Houses. A giant Paul Bunyan, still there, originally greeted visitors to the Paul Bunyan Wood Center, where logs were crafted into finished products. Admission was just 25 cents for kids, $1 for adults, and circus acts became part of the attraction. In 1984, the first water slide was added, and by 1988, the park's name was expanded to Enchanted Forest/Water Safari. Now with thirty-one water rides, it's New York's largest water theme park.

Magic Forest in Lake George opened in 1963 to catch New Yorkers on their way to the Adirondacks. A wooded trail has dozens of fairy-tale figures. In Latham, Hoffman's Playland has five adult rides and thirteen kiddie rides and has been open since 1952.

Just south of the Connecticut border, in Rye, New York, is another Playland, this one along

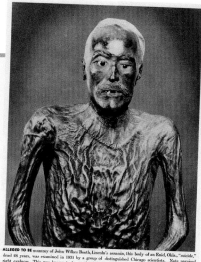

The Fairgrounds in Allentown, Pennsylvania, a block from the house where I grew up, is home to the weeklong Great Allentown Fair. In the late 1950s, an attraction near the end of the midway caught my eye as I made my way past my favorite rides, the Bullet and the Round-Up, and the freak shows where Schlitzie the Pinhead shared the stage with a man who drove a framing nail up his nose. I bought a ticket to see the mummy of John Wilkes Booth. This shriveled leathery carcass, which had been touring carnivals for decades, was displayed by a former Tattooed Man. Though I learned later that it was someone else's body, when I was ten this experience left an indelible mark and inspired a forty-year study of Lincoln's assassination.

—RICHARD J. S. GUTMAN, author of *American Diner: Then and Now*

The mummy touted as John Wilkes Booth turned out to be a fraud, but not before thrilling crowds as a sideshow attraction. It was pictured in the September 2, 1941, issue of *PIC*. RICHARD J. S. GUTMAN

the beaches of Long Island Sound. By the end of the nineteenth century, locals concerned by the seashore's bawdy amusements and rowdy crowds petitioned the Westchester County Park Commission to redevelop the area. In 1927, the commission bought and razed two parks and built Playland on the site, making it America's first planned amusement park. Opened in 1928, it also remains the country's only government-owned-and-operated amusement park. Seven

The Boardwalk and bathhouse at Rye Playland overlook Long Island Sound. The park was built in 1928 as an antidote to more rowdy beachfront resorts. It was the country's first planned amusement park, and remains the only one built and operated by a government entity.

FAN FAVORITE

The shores of New York's Oneida Lake are home to the little-known Sylvan Beach Amusement Park. It is a nostalgic trip back to the shore parks of yesteryear, with its collection of classic rides, games, and food. LaffLand, a fifty-year-old dark ride, alone is worth the trip to experience one of the oldest such attractions in the United States, and likely the only one that contains most of the original stunts that have entertained generations of riders since it was first constructed.

A collection of traditional kiddie rides along with some old favorite adult rides like the Roll-O-Plane, Loop-O-Plane, Crazy Daisy, Tilt-A-Whirl, and bumper cars combine with classic games such as Fascination and Skee-Ball to bring back memories of the old days. The park also has the largest roller coaster in Central New York, which is in fact the *only* roller coaster in central New York!

—RICK DAVIS, co-founder of Darkride and
Funhouse Enthusiasts

LaffLand, entertaining at Sylvan Beach since 1954.
RICK DAVIS

pre-1930 rides remain, including the carousel with an 1890s band organ and sixty-six hand-painted horses and chariots carved in 1915. The Derby Racer, one of only two left, is similar to a carousel but has horses actually racing for position as the ride spins at twenty-five miles per hour. The Dragon Coaster, from 1929, shoots riders out the dragon's fire-breathing mouth, and running beneath it, the Old Mill follows the coaster's layout via water. It also has a bathhouse, Ice Casino with three skating rinks, and more than fifty rides. The park was designed in Art Deco and Spanish Revival, and many buildings retain their architectural details. Playland became a national historic landmark in 1987, and like all good classic parks, it does not charge admission.

Sylvan Beach Amusement Park, along the eastern shore of Oneida Lake in New York, is part of the Sylvan-Verona Beach Resort Area, offering beaches, boating, fishing, and camping. The park was founded in the late nineteenth century but grew very slowly. Many of the two dozen or so

rides are older. The LaffLand dark ride was installed in a bathhouse that had been out over the lake; the narrow building was split in two, rolled inland, and reassembled with the halves side by side to fit the ride. It is among the most popular of the genre—not the most shocking, but a well-maintained ride with interesting stunts, gags, and sound effects.

The best-known park in New York State is really a grouping of amusements at the southern tip of Brooklyn. Coney Island has changed greatly over the past century, peaking in the 1920s and declining after World War II, but recent efforts and a new minor-league ballpark are helping revive the area, which remains an old-fashioned escape for New Yorkers. The major amusement parks—Dreamland, Luna Park, and Steeplechase—are long gone, but remnants survive, such as the spindly 1939 Parachute Jump, where riders were lifted 190 feet and then dropped using guy-wired parachutes; it's been completely rebuilt but stands in limbo as to whether it will again carry passengers.

Astroland lies just beyond the boardwalk at Coney Island, with Dino's Wonder Wheel looming over it at left.

FAN FAVORITE

In the 1970s, my father took me to a quirky but interesting tourist attraction near our home. Holy Land U.S.A., atop Pine Hill in Waterbury, Connecticut, was the vision of local lawyer John Greco and was built in the late 1950s by volunteers, including my grandfather and great-uncle. It was a miniature Bethlehem of sorts, and a popular tourist destination for many years, drawing much attention with its large, illuminated cross and Hollywood-style sign. I have some vague memories of Holy Land, mainly of the climb up and the miniature buildings.

I visited my grandmother last year, and as she lives minutes away from the site of Holy Land, I went there to look around. Sadly, it has long been closed and is in a bad state of disrepair, with an uncertain future. But my mom gave me some slides of Holy Land U.S.A. taken by her uncle, Donald Lucian, back in the 1950s and 1960s. Among them were photos of the attraction when it was new and some of its construction.

—JENNIFER BREMER, www.roadtripmemories.com

The Holy Land miniature village in Waterbury, Connecticut, has sat abandoned for years.

49

Coney Island is filled with arcades, food stands, gift shops, and of course, the Boardwalk. For a smaller, kid-oriented place, try tiny Nellie Bly Park, which changed hands in 2005 after forty years with the same family. The new family is striving to upgrade and reopen the city-owned three-acre lot. Astroland has about a dozen rides for kids and as many for adults, such as a pirate ship, bumper cars, and Dante's Inferno dark ride. There are three arcades. Since 1975, Astroland has operated the Cyclone, the most famous wooden coaster, built in 1927. The small space it had to fit into forced its builder to make the drops steep and the turns tight. It influenced many others, and the operators claim seven copies are still operating around the world.

Also at Coney Island, Deno's Wonder Wheel Amusement Park is named for Greek immigrant Denos Vourderis. He managed Ward's kiddie park in the 1960s and became owner in 1981. Two years later, he acquired a couple adjacent rides. The 150-foot-tall Wonder Wheel was built in 1920, the steel forged right on-site. The amazing part is not the Ferris-wheel-like eight stationary cars, but sixteen swinging cages that coast from the outer circumference toward the center of the wheel and back. The other, the Spook-A-Rama, opened in 1955 and remains probably the longest dark ride ever with more than a quarter mile of track, four times the normal length. There are

three other rides for adults and seventeen for kids. There is no fee to walk around the park.

Another must at Coney Island is Nathan's Famous at Surf and Stillwell Avenues, which draws big crowds for its hot dogs and fries. It has locations across the country, but fans swear by this one, where Nathan Handwerker launched his business in 1916. He had worked for Charles Feltman, who is said to have conceived the hot dog—a Vienna sausage in a sliced roll—as a food to sell easily from a push cart. Nathan's is best known for its annual hot-dog-eating contest every Fourth of July.

Sideshows by the Seashore entertains visitors to Coney Island with a ten-in-one circus sideshow attraction. Current cast members include Insectavora, Bambi the Mermaid, the Great Fredini, Helen Melon, and the Twisted Shockmeister.

The nonprofit Coney Island USA operates the Coney Island Museum and Sideshows by the Seashore and hosts the annual Mermaid Parade. The 1917 building that houses the museum, shows, and visitors center is decorated inside and out with canvas sideshow banners. Current cast members include Insectavora, Bambi the Mermaid, the Great Fredini, Helen Melon, and the Twisted Shockmeister.

The Coney Island name was widely adapted by other parks, not to mention hot-dog stands. A Coney Island park near Cincinnati dates to 1886 but has had its ups and downs. A 1937 flood submerged the park in twenty-eight feet of water, nearly destroying it. Other floods caused further damage, but in 1969, the park was bought by the owner of the Hanna-Barbera cartoon characters, who decided to relocate and develop a theme park called King's Island. Coney Island closed after 1971, but small parts of the park hung on, and in 1987, rides were added again. There are now more than twenty rides and admission is free.

Very little has changed over half a century at The Kiddie Park in San Antonio, Texas, and that's the way management and customers like it— attendance increases each year. It has ten rides for kids, including little boats, helicopters, and planes mounted with machine guns.

Another vintage Texas park, which has grown to be the third largest in the state, is Wonderland in Amarillo. In 1951, Paul Roads moved his family here to pursue his dream of owning a park. On August 12, Kiddie Land opened with a boat ride, car ride, and Little Dipper coaster. With help from his in-laws, Roads spent the next decade working eight hours a day at a welding job before going to work at the park in the evening. After a doctor advised him to slow down, he left his day job, renamed the park Wonderland, and began expanding with bigger rides. Children and now grandchildren manage the park.

The Kiddie Park in Bartlesville, Oklahoma, also keeps up the tradition of free admission, with fees for each ride. The park, founded in 1947, has grown to sixteen rides for children age twelve and under. It is run by the Bartlesville Playground

Association, a nonprofit organization whose sole purpose is to operate and manage the Kiddie Park. Operation is funded by contributions, ticket sales, and concessions.

Lakeside Amusement Park in Denver pales in size and amenities to the nearby Six Flags Elitch Gardens, but fans know Lakeside is way cooler, has short lines, and is a lot more affordable. And though Elitch claims roots to 1890, it's only been at its current site since 1995, while Lakeside traces its history to 1908, when it opened as White City, a

---

FAN FAVORITE

The Big Peach is a 135-foot-tall water tank shaped and painted like a ripe peach and plunked alongside I-85 in Gaffney, South Carolina. Seen above the trees, it can look like a hovering extraterrestrial spaceship. From other angles, at other times, it can look like a sun rising above the mobile-home dealer on the frontage road or a fat, full moon too heavy to make it above the horizon. I especially enjoy the way it picks up on the qualities of the delicious paintings of peaches on the roadside fruit stands of the area. Cezanne and his peaches have nothing on those local painters. The Big Peach is the modern variation of the great American tradition of celebrating local products—oranges, apples, cotton, peanuts, pigs or mules—with landmarks and festivals.

It also serves as a hopeful testimonial that roadside attractions are not just the province of individual entrepreneurs and small businesses. Local government and boosters built this one. The Big Peach was dreamed up by Jack Millwood, a former undertaker and insurance agent who was chairman of the public works department in the 1970s. Engineers and steel fabricators built it, and it won an award from the steel association. It holds the hope of the future where the great tradition of boosting local products is also a vital part of the infrastructure.

—PHIL PATTON, author of *Open Road* and *Dreamland* and writer for the *New York Times*, philpatton.com

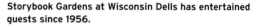

The Tower of Jewels rises 150 feet over Lakeside Amusement Park in Denver. Built for the park's 1908 opening, the building originally housed a casino.

nod to its lighting. Admission is $2 but includes a 50-cent coupon for rides. The park has fifteen kiddie rides and others from the 1940s, such as the Cyclone coaster, the Autoskooter, Skoota Boats, and Hurricane. The merry-go-round is as old as the park itself. Two steam trains from the 1904 St. Louis World's Fair circle Lake Rhoda, named for the owner by her father, who turned the park around during the Depression.

The Santa Cruz Beach Boardwalk is a half-mile vintage amusement park along the Pacific Coast with thirty-four rides, including two national historic landmarks—a 1911 carousel and 1924 Giant Dipper roller coaster—next to a mile-long beach. The carousel features one of the few remaining ring machines. Riders on the outside horses can grab a steel ring and try to throw it into a clown's mouth; success brings sounds and flashing lights.

Cypress Gardens in Winter Haven, Florida, was started in 1936 as a dream garden. Carved from a swamp and known for its 8,000 varieties

Storybook Gardens at Wisconsin Dells has entertained guests since 1956.

of flowers, it became famous for water-ski shows and young ladies dressed as southern belles. But it couldn't compete with the big attractions in Orlando. After closing in 2003, it was purchased by the owner of Wild Adventures in Valdosta, Georgia, the nation's largest privately owned park. Cypress Gardens has now been re-created as an amusement park, with four roller coasters and dozens of other rides, concerts, and events. Plans for the park include rebuilding the 1963 Starliner coaster from Miracle Strip amusement park, which closed in 2004. The Starliner is one of eleven designed by the famous John Allen that still survives.

Many arcade amusements, especially coin-op machines that play music or a game, have been preserved at Musee Mecanique, or "mechanical museum," at Fisherman's Wharf in San Francisco. The museum opened in the 1920s in Playland at the Beach, which by the 1950s had become the largest year-round amusement park in the United States. When the park closed in 1972, the museum moved to the Cliff House restaurant, then to its

The entrance to Story Land in Glen, New Hampshire, has always been through a Crooked House, this one from 1954. The cutout man on the roof is the storyteller.

Flintstones Bedrock City in South Dakota still sells these vivid plates made for the park's 1966 opening.

current site in 2002. The late Edward Galland Zelinsky began acquiring mechanical things at age eleven, and he eventually amassed the largest private machine collection. Zelinsky's son Daniel continues the tradition. Admission is free, but bring lots of change for the machines.

Many of the surviving older parks were launched during the Baby Boom of the 1950s. A popular trend was the fairy-tale park, which quickly spread across the country but faded by the 1970s. Stoney Morrell Jr. says the inspiration for Story Land in New Hampshire came to his parents, Bob and Ruth, from a woman they met in Germany while serving in the U.S. Army in the early 1950s. The woman suggested they build a village to house the fairy-tale dolls she made. They expanded the idea to have the characters come to

I first realized that I was addicted to roadside oddities about fifteen years ago, during a long drive through the empty prairies of central North Dakota. Passing near the little town of Pettibone, I noticed the most incongruous thing possible in that setting: a tall, octagonal, silver pagoda, ringed with balconies and topped with an onion dome gleaming in the late-afternoon sun.

As I walked around with my camera, I was approached by the tower's creator, a septuagenarian named Henry. He'd built the thing with lumber from a

salvaged grain elevator and offered to give me a tour. Henry's pagoda was eighty-two feet high and filled with eight stories of stuff: Formica floor tiles, old carpet samples, 45-rpm records, toys salvaged from junkyards. Each level had its own theme. On the top floor, I bravely climbed a ladder leading to a hatchway in the dome and saw a view of the prairies that was nothing short of magnificent.

Nearby was a workshop filled with exquisite miniatures Henry had created, and his then current project reposed in the yard—a giant Hereford bull whose interior was reached by a stairway entering through the creature's gullet. It was all amazing and surreal, and I've been looking for cool roadside creations ever since.

Sadly, the Pettibone Pagoda is no longer with us. Henry died in 1995, and four years later the whole thing toppled over in a giant Dakota windstorm. When I visited later, bits of the ruined pagoda were strewn over most of a city block, and the roof of Henry's workshop had collapsed. Last I heard, only the giant Hereford was still around, sitting in front of a bar in the little town of Buchanan. It's in rough shape, decaying and vandalized, and suffering the aftereffects of the bar owner's attempt to carve a stage into its torso. The treasures of the world can indeed be fleeting.

—MARK HUFSTETLER, architectural historian, Bozeman, Montana

The Pettibone Pagoda, between Bismarck and Fargo, North Dakota, around 1980. ANNA AND HOWARD HUFSTETLER

life and opened the park in 1954. The only ride then was a real fire engine. Like so many of the surviving small parks, Stoney says the goal was to provide a clean, courteous, and relaxing environment for families.

Somewhat similar are the parks built around the Flintstones characters. The first one, in Custer, South Dakota, opened in 1966 and is still going strong, drawing families visiting nearby Mount Rushmore. Another opened six years later in Valle, Arizona, and attracts families on their way to the Grand Canyon. Both re-create the buildings of Bedrock and feature oversize characters. Two parks also opened in British Columbia but were ordered to stop using the licensed characters; one in Kelowna was demolished in 1998, but the other in Chilliwack was rethemed in 1994 as Dinoland, now Dinotown Jurassic Theme Park, North America's only cartoon dinosaur town.

The Midwest has long been home to larger-than-life characters. Many towns have latched on to *The Wizard of Oz* theme to lure tourists. Most are in Kansas, Dorothy's home state, but Aberdeen, South Dakota, has the largest park devoted to the fantasy stories. From 1888 to 1891, Aberdeen was home to *The Wonderful Wizard of Oz* author L. Frank Baum. The town's Storybook Land is a free park filled with fairy-tale characters, and a new ten-acre portion is devoted to the characters from Oz.

Just as well known, but without a popular movie or theme song, is legendary lumberjack Paul Bunyan. He was one of the original draws to New York's Enchanted Forest and remains the main attraction at Paul Bunyan Land, east of Brainerd, Minnesota. When the park opened in town in 1950, it was called Paul Bunyan Playground, a nickname the town itself had earned after starting a Paul Bunyan Days Parade in 1935. The park featured an animated thirty-six-foot-tall Paul, built for the 1948 Chicago Railroad Fair. After the park closed in 2003, Babe was relocated to the nearby Paul Bunyan Bowl bowling alley, where the ox has been paired with a Muffler Man–style Paul. The original Paul and the rides moved east of town to This Old Farm Pioneer Vil-

Paul Bunyan Land at This Old Farm Pioneer Village in Brainerd, Minnesota, also features Paul's oversize mailbox and Sport, his reversible dog.

lage. Paul continues to move his head, mouth, and arms while talking to visitors. Kids are especially surprised when, through the magic of helpful ticket takers, Paul greets them by name. Next to

The Land of Oz in Aberdeen, South Dakota, honors onetime resident L. Frank Baum, author of the fantasy books. MARK HUFSTETLER

him is Sport the reversible dog. Legend has it that when a logger accidentally cut the dog in two, his hind legs were sewn back on upside down. Sport didn't mind—when he tired from running on his front legs, he'd flip over and run on his back legs.

The most famous statues of Paul Bunyan and Babe are to the north in Bemidji, but the Brainerd region goes all out in its Paul publicity. A water tower is said to be Paul's flashlight, and standing next to it are a smaller Paul and Babe. A new Paul sits outside the Brainerd Lakes Area Welcome Center on MN 371 South. Paul's wooden baby shoe can be found inside the Pine River Information Center, a wooden ax sits outside Ace Hard-

ware in Crosslake, and his fishing bobber, another water tower, is in Pequot Lakes.

The original part of This Old Farm Pioneer Village features more than thirty century-old buildings, including a blacksmith shop, saloon, dentist office, and sawmill, along with antique cars. Paul and Babe make another appearance with antique buildings at the Paul Bunyan Logging Camp at Carson Park in Eau Claire, Wisconsin. The town, at the junction of the Chippewa and Eau Claire Rivers, attracted lumbermills in the late 1800s, and the pine lumber industry flourished. The camp has an interpretive center and other buildings authentic to the 1900s logging era, plus fiber-

FAN FAVORITE

My grandfather rarely left the house without his worn cowboy boots and ten-gallon feathered hat. For a steelworker from Uniontown, Pennsylvania, this was an unexpected uniform. Granddaddy Evans *was* the cowboy he emulated: a B-17 bomber pilot, consummate Johnny Cash fan, and lifelong western traveler. He left behind a well-documented life of family excursions in Kodak slides. It was with visions of his 1974 stop in Jackson, Wyoming, that I first entered the Million Dollar Cowboy Bar.

Signs light the night in Jackson Hole, Wyoming.
JENNIFER BARON

The dazzling display of western memorabilia was almost jarring: knobbled pine interiors, saddle bar stools, and lacquered, paint-by-number-style cowboy murals. Spurs and chaps hung in place of light fixtures, and massive dioramas featured predator-meets-prey confrontations between stuffed timber wolves, mountain lions, and bighorn sheep. An ornate bar inlaid with 624 silver dollars ran above a monogrammed red carpet fabricated in London.

Founded by Ben Goe, the bar has welcomed thirsty patrons since 1937. The huge double-faced sign, installed in 1953, is one of the tallest visual markers in a town with a sternly enforced building code. The "million dollar" tag was added at this time as a nod to the cost of renovations after a gas heater explosion damaged the building.

Country music legends Waylon Jennings, Hoyt Axton, Glen Campbell, Tanya Tucker, and Willie Nelson have graced its stage, and many notables such as Harrison Ford, Kevin Costner, Jimmy Connors, and the late JFK Jr. have visited. It was the setting for a scene in Clint Eastwood's *Every Which Way But Loose* and a premier party for *Brokeback Mountain*.

Every summer night at 6 P.M., the town re-creates a western shoot-out for families who spill onto wooden sidewalks. For those with more spirit, the Cowboy Bar hosts waltz and two-step lessons every Thursday.

—JENNIFER BARON, co-founder of the Pittsburgh Signs Project, pittsburghsigns.org

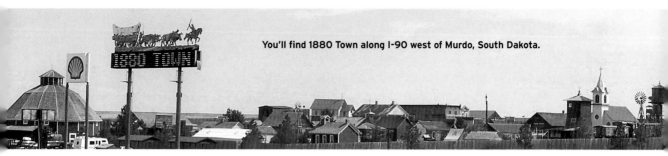

You'll find 1880 Town along I-90 west of Murdo, South Dakota.

glass statues of the famous duo. When Paul was knocked over in 2002, locals rallied to repair the figures; Kim Nessel, battalion chief for Eau Claire Fire Department Station No. 2, even took time off from his job to help.

Gatherings of frontier buildings and museums of rural life seem especially common across the Great Plains. The long stretches, the need to attract people, and the high survival rate of rural buildings inspired frontier towns or agricultural museums along most every highway. But similar attractions are also found throughout the United States. Manitou Springs, Colorado, has the Flying W Ranch, as well as Buckskin Joe Frontier Town and Railway. Three such sites are found in western North Carolina, in Boone, Franklin, and Maggie Valley. Most famous is Alamo Village, the movie set John Wayne built in Texas to recreate the Alamo for his 1960 movie about the famous battle. There are no false fronts; all the buildings are full-size reproductions in board and batten or adobe. The "Waynamo," as it's also called, has since served as a set for more than 200 other films.

In South Dakota, 1880 Town began as a movie set but was never used as such by the builders. It now survives as a tourist attraction, with more than thirty buildings and numerous props from the Kevin Costner movie *Dances with Wolves*, including a tent, sod house, Timmons's freight wagons, and even one of the horses.

Frontier Village in Jamestown, North Dakota, has a collection of regional rural buildings, including a post office and the state's oldest grocery store. It all started in 1959 with the construction of a sixty-ton concrete buffalo by local sign shop owner Harold Newman as a way to draw visitors to the town. It led to the assemblage of eighteen buildings and has grown to include a museum, gift shop, and herd of buffalo with a rare albino named White Cloud.

Wild West City in New Jersey is geared more toward kids. The 1956 park is an authentic reproduction of Dodge City in the 1880s. Every fifteen minutes you will see a performance of a holdup, gunfight, or Pony Express rider galloping into town. But the park emphasizes that its portrayals are historical reenactments and that it does not advocate violence.

Many of these sites opened in the 1950s, when the nation was wild for the West, but their popularity faded along with the trend in the 1970s. Frontier Town opened on July 4, 1952, in the town

This forty-six-foot-long buffalo in Jamestown, North Dakota, inspired the construction of Frontier Village and National Buffalo Museum. BUFFALO CITY TOURISM FOUNDATION

FAN FAVORITE

Gibsonton is ten miles south of Tampa but miles farther from anything ordinary. The summer (and for many, permanent) home of many in the carnival industry, "Gibtown" is a forgotten land of thrills and magic.

The Giant's Camp Restaurant, open twenty-four hours, is a wonderful starting point. Inside, learn the history of the late Al "Giant" Tomaini and his wife, Jeanie "Half Woman," while enjoying the good food.

Savoring my breakfast with huge homemade biscuits, I imagined the days of yore when Lobster Boy, the Human Blockhead, and Monkey Girl and her husband, Alligator Man, were regulars at this place.

Take time to enjoy the artwork on the outside walls of the fascinating Showtown restaurant and bar. You will surely find a few carnies inside, along with friendly conversation and spirits. The bartenders will gladly provide stories about this magical village and suggest additional sites to visit. The interior artwork evokes a bygone era of carnival splendor. Thanks to friendly zoning laws in Gibtown, also called Showtown USA, carnies can keep wild animals and carnival rides on their property.

Be sure to check out the Gibtown Showman's Club, where donations for a carnival museum will help preserve the town's colorful, vibrant history.

—SHARI PAGLIA, photographer and roadside enthusiast

Showtown's colorful facade is one of many cool places to see in Gibtown, Florida. SHARI PAGLIA

of North Hudson in the Adirondacks. Despite its name, it became an Old West theme park when the men's frontier costumes failed to arrive and cowboy outfits were substituted. It closed in 1998 after attendance declined and was auctioned off in 2004. Similarly, Guntown Mountain in Cave City, Kentucky, featured gunfights among Wild West buildings, but it closed after the 2005 season. The rides were auctioned off, though the chair lift and haunted house remain, as well as the general store and gift shop at the base of the mountain. One of the best-known sites to close recently was the Ponderosa Ranch, based on the TV show *Bonanza*, which ran from 1959 to 1973. Some scenes were actually filmed there, and it became a mecca for fans of the show and other western dramas of the era. Located near Lake Tahoe, Nevada, the land became valuable and was sold for redevelopment.

Wrapping up our amusing-places excursion is Gibsonton, Florida, where many sideshow performers spend the winter. Ten miles south of Tampa, Gibtown began in 1924 when the Giant's Camp Restaurant was opened by Al "The Giant" Tomaini, who stood eight feet, four and a half inches, and his wife, Jeanie, who, having no legs, was only two feet, six inches. Other performers who settled here had such features as webbed fingers or atypical hair growth. Modern health care has reduced their numbers in general, and today Gibtown features stunt performers and yards filled with carnival equipment.

SPOTLIGHT ON
Christmas Parks

Christmas-themed parks were especially popular during the Baby Boom years. A lot of these parks have since closed or expanded to reach a wider year-round demographic by including other holidays, many joining the haunted-house frenzy at Halloween. A few of the vintage parks survive, however, throwbacks to the day they opened.

The park credited with starting the fad, and the first in fact to be called a theme park, is Santa's Workshop in New York State. Lake Placid businessman Julian Reiss got the idea when his daughter asked him to take her to Santa's summer home. His park opened on July 1, 1949, and within a couple years, Walt Disney company Imagineers began visiting to get ideas for a theme park of their own. The park was a huge hit and even got its own zip code in 1953. One of the most memorable features is an icy white North Pole frozen year-round. When the founding family retired in 2001, the park soon ran into trouble under a new owner and closed briefly. In 2002, Doug Waterbury purchased it and has launched a five-year restoration. Be sure to visit and feed the reindeer, direct descendants of the original

Fresh gingerbread cookies from the Sugar 'N Spice Bake Shop, at Santa's Village, New Hampshire. The cookies are famous, and kids can decorate their own.
SANTA'S VILLAGE

herd flown in from Golovan, Alaska, for the park's opening in 1953.

Another long-standing park is Santa's Village in New Hampshire. Elaine Dubois Gainer, whose parents founded it, told us about growing up at the park:

I was three years old when my folks began the park. My mom and dad had their own business in Lancaster, but the chemicals involved in dry cleaning were getting to my dad. He knew he'd have to find something else to do. That was 1952. At that time, amusement parks were not considered respectable ventures. Most parks were carnival-like in nature, and no self-respecting businessman or woman would dare risk an already successful business for an amusement park.

But Norm and Cecile Dubois were not typical businesspeople. By the early 1950s, they envisioned something unique to the area—a family amusement park. They also recognized the beauty of Jefferson, especially a sixteen-acre

Santa Claus and the "North Pole" at Santa's Workshop in New York State's Adirondacks. SANTA'S WORKSHOP

piece of land occupied by a grove of fir trees. As we drove past the land, a young fawn jumped out of the woods into the road in front of our car. When I asked what it was, my dad told me it was one of Santa's reindeer.

My parents did not believe in coincidence. It had to be fate that a Christmas theme park should rest on that parcel of land. It wasn't long after they signed the papers on the land that they began to construct the first buildings, consisting of an entrance, Santa's Home, Souvenir Shop, Toy Shop, and Post Office. They opened the gates for the first guests on Father's Day, 1953.

She also emphasizes that Santa's helpers, the employees, are who make it all possible. Grandchildren now are involved in the operation, and all are proud of the original buildings, family atmosphere, and slower pace.

The Santa park trend spread southward to Cherokee, North Carolina, and westward to Indiana. In Cherokee, Santa's Land Park and Zoo offers the customary Santa's House plus the Rudolph-the-Red-Nosed-Reindeer-themed Rudicoaster, magic shows at the Jingle Bell Theater, and some cool souvenirs, such as green felt elf hats. Besides reindeer, kids can visit—and sometimes pet or feed—monkeys, sheep, llamas, turkeys, rabbits, pigs, peacocks, and baby bears and tigers. Too bad it's closed in December.

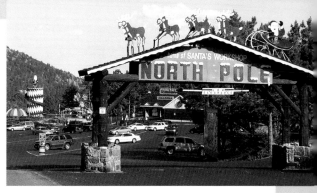

Santa's Workshop at the North Pole, on the way up Pikes Peak in Colorado.

In Indiana, Holiday World and Splashin' Safari opened on August 3, 1946, as Santa Claus Land. It's located in the town of Santa Claus, and most everything here has a Yuletide theme, from Christmas Boulevard to Lake Rudolph. The park's name changed in 1984 when its themes expanded to include other holidays. It now has four sections: Christmas, Halloween, Fourth of July, and Thanksgiving. The park is repeatedly voted the friendliest and cleanest in the world by readers of *Amusement Today*. The third generation of family members now operate the ever-growing park.

Far to the west in Colorado is one more of the precious parks, Santa's Workshop in the town of North Pole. The announcement in 1955 stated that it would be identical to Santa's Workshop in Lake Placid. It opened the next summer with puppet shows, storybook characters, and roaming animals as the main attractions. Rides were added in 1958, and the park has continued to expand, although it retains a small scale and friendly atmosphere. When we needed a bandage, the park's owner was manning the first-aid station.

Not every Christmas-themed park has a happy ending. Santa's Village Amusement Park in East Dundee, outside Chicago, was the first theme-park franchise. Opened in 1959, this was the third location, preceded by Skyforest (1955–98) and Scotts Valley (1957–79), both in California. Like other Christmas parks, it contained all the usual buildings and attractions, such as a frozen North Pole. The park was hugely popular and beloved by the community, but operators failed to pay taxes and water bills in recent years. Fans and business leaders tried desperately throughout 2006 to resurrect the park, but by October the contents were auctioned off.

The Pleasureland area at Santa Claus Land, around 1955. This is now Rudolph's Reindeer Ranch in the Christmas section of Holiday World in Santa Claus, Indiana. HOLIDAY WORLD AND SPLASHIN' SAFARI

CHAPTER 4

WILD THINGS

Roadside attractions that feature wildlife face tough challenges. Many people today have seen even the most exotic animals on TV or in books. The Internet, video editing, and electronic devices continually ramp up the speed and inten-

Florida's many attractions are well represented in old and new brochures. Here are vintage rack cards from Monkey Jungle, Parrot Jungle, and Musa Isle, all in Miami.

sity of sensory stimulation. So when deciding among entertainment options, potential customers increasingly look past animal parks and petting zoos for bigger, faster, and louder thrills. Recent decades have also seen people's perception of animal habitats evolve so that they now view cramped concrete cages as inadequate and cruel. While customers may be disheartened at such displays, activists go much further, campaigning for better conditions that may be justified but not financially possible in a declining marketplace. The result is that almost every roadside attraction that featured animals has closed. A few remade the habitats and reinvented themselves as educational exhibits.

Florida quickly benefited from the flow of automobile tourists in the mid-twentieth century, and many attractions featured exotic wildlife. Among them were St. Augustine Alligator Farm, McKee Jungle Gardens, Ross Allen Reptile Institute, Nature's Giant Fish Bowl, Everglades Wonder Gardens, Marine Studios, Sarasota Jungle Gardens, Miami Serpentarium and Seaquarium, Bartlett's Deer Ranch, Monkey Jungle, and Parrot Jungle.

North of Tampa, the Chimp Farm closed a few years ago after accusations of inferior facilities, but new owners have since been trying to remake it. It was founded by Bob and Anna Mae Noell, who crossed the country with Noell's Ark Gorilla Show, in which locals boxed with the animals. (They had only chimpanzees, but the public wanted gorillas, so that's what they called it.) In 1954, they bought the Alligator Farm and converted it to the Chimp Farm. Caretakers ran it

The Pymatuning Spillway is hard to explain to someone who's never been there. It's in a state park in northwestern Pennsylvania, just south of the town of Linesville on the road to Hartstown. People gather here to gawk and throw stale bread at thousands of big, hungry carp. The fish were imported from Germany and have grown huge on high-carb diets. Nearby, roadside shops sell old bread to feed the fish. People also feed the ducks that walk across the fish's backs.

Pymatuning is a lovely man-made lake, a reservoir created by a dam built near Jamestown in 1934. The upper part of the lake is two feet higher than the rest, and water often flows to the lower part over this old concrete spillway. Fish probably were first attracted here because the water coming over the spillway has lots of gill-enriching oxygen. And people must have noticed the carp gathering, and maybe someone dropped a sandwich. Who knows?

Now it often looks as if there's little water in the Spillway. It's just gargantuan fish, splashing, mouths open, fighting for bread. And everyone loves it. You can't look away.

—RICK SEBAK, producer and narrator of *Pennsylvania Diners and Other Roadside Restaurants*, *A Hot Dog Program*, and other slightly wacky documentaries made by WQED Multimedia Pittsburgh for PBS

Feeding the fish at Linesville, Pennsylvania.

during summers while they went on the road. They concentrated on caring for abandoned animals, mostly apes and monkeys, but by the 1990s, the type of cage they had was considered inhumane. People for the Ethical Treatment of Animals (PETA) called the Chimp Farm "one of the worst roadside zoos in the country." Writing in 1994 and once posted online by her grandson, Anna Mae distinguished between their place and fly-by-night operations:

> Most such operators had a flatbed truck and a travel trailer. The truck would usually be loaded to capacity with small cages containing the cheapest possible animals; raccoons, opossums, fox, badger, ground hog, prairie dogs, wolf, etc. . . . Often as not it was only a man & wife running it. She would act as a guide for the mother and children while her consort would call the man back into an alcove and work the "shell game" or "three card monte" on him. If they made a big "score" and "cleaned" the man before the police could arrive, the car, truck, and trailer were gone. Sometimes the animals might even be abandoned. Please don't call us a "roadside zoo." We can't load our animals and run away. Our walls & cages are cement and have been here since 1954. This is a "Retirement Home for Aging Primates."

By 1999, the Chimp Farm's cement cages led to the attraction's forced closure. The site was converted to the nonprofit Suncoast Primate Sanctuary, relying solely on donations and volunteers. Its website lists the many ongoing expenses, from oatmeal to electricity as well as

$250,000 in debt remaining from building the new Great Ape Habitat. The sanctuary takes in abused or abandoned animals, including chimpanzees, orangutans, reptiles, and even a retired circus bear, and expects to reopen to the public. Currently only members who pay an annual fee can visit, or one can join the 150 volunteers who are making the site a state-of-the-art retirement home for animals.

Monkey Jungle in Miami likewise has been under decades of family ownership and has also seen its share of protestors. The setting here, though, is very different, as indicated by its motto: "Where Humans Are Caged and Monkeys Run Wild!" The roots of the thirty-acre wildlife park go back to 1933, when animal behaviorist Joseph DuMond released six Java monkeys into the dense South Florida hammock, a term referring to land slightly above the swamps. That troup has grown to more than eighty, and thirty other primate species are represented, including gibbons, guenons, and spider monkeys.

Monkey Jungle also served as inspiration for another Florida attraction. Austrian immigrant Franz Scherr loved nature, and after a talk with Joseph DuMond, he started Parrot Jungle by renting twenty acres of hammock land south of Miami for $25 per year. He wanted his birds to fly free, and though few believed they would with the park, the birds did just that. Opening in 1936, the attraction was hugely popular, even visited by Winston Churchill. (There's a famous photo with a parrot on his arm.) Parrot Jungle even supplied the pink flamingos at the opening of *Miami Vice*. With upscale housing surrounding the site, it moved to Watson Island in 2003, and the old site was remade as Pinecrest Gardens municipal park. The new Parrot Jungle Island has been called "overly fabricated" by Frommer's, but fans of the old park will still find roller-skating cockatoos and card-playing macaws, plus 1,100 tropical birds, 2,000 varieties of plants and flowers, and animals ranging from tigers to orangutans. Even the Serpentarium, a nearby popular attraction from the 1940s through 1980s, has been revived at the new site, with Crocosaurus, a

As we made our way around Florida in the 1990s, even the 1930s botanical attraction Sunken Gardens, in St. Petersburg, advertised alligators.

twenty-foot-long saltwater crocodile, as the star. And the birds still fly free.

For an experience (and pricing) more like parks of old, head south to Gatorama, west of Lake Okeechobee. Started in 1957, the fifteen-acre attraction with a 1,000-foot-long covered walkway features monkeys, peacocks, geese, 250 crocodiles (representing six species), and of course, gators—about 3,000 of them. It is now run by the daughter of the family that purchased it in 1986, and the third generation is helping too. They harvest about 1,000 gators per year for their hides and meat; in fact, it's the only alligator farm that ships meat directly to consumers. That's one way to stay afloat while most cross-state traffic now takes I-75.

Gatorland near Orlando traces its roots to 1947, when Owen Godwin Sr. bought 16 rural acres along Routes 17/92 and 441 in Kissimmee

My husband, Rob, and I flew into Toronto in February 2005. Probably its most famous attraction is the CN Tower, the tallest building in the world. Rising 1,815 feet, it's an incredible sight. When our taxi pulled up to the curb, we stepped out and looked straight up. The tower is so tall you feel as if you have to do a backbend in order to see all the way to the top.

Once inside, you can take a tour providing a short history lesson on some the world's other tallest buildings. Then the real fun begins as you enter the elevator. Not only is it incredibly fast, but it also has a glass front and travels on the outside of the building. What a ride! My ears were popping the whole way up.

When you reach the top, the platform gives you an incredible 360-degree view of Toronto and way beyond. Rob and I enjoyed a romantic lunch; then we headed over to the tower's glass floor—one of the most popular attractions in the building. It was really a funny scene. Not confident with the strength of the floor, a lot of people just quickly walk across it. Others lean over to look down but don't dare put any weight on it. At first I only stepped on and off quickly. After doing this a couple times, I finally worked up the nerve to put my full weight on it.

After playing around a while and admiring the view one last time, we needed to come back down to earth. To properly finish our touristy day, we stopped at the gift shop on the way out to pick up some souvenirs.

—AMBER J. MARIANO, winner of *Survivor All-Stars*
and contestant on *The Amazing Race 7* and *11*

Amazing Race participants Amber and Rob Mariano, perhaps better known for their *Survivor* appearances, had some fun at Orlando's Gatorland in 2004.

to open a park, though no one else thought people would pay for what they could see all around for free. At first he called it the Florida Wildlife Institute and featured gator wrestling by Seminole Indians, but he soon changed the name to the more tourist-drawing Snake Village and Alligator Farm. To pay for improvements, Godwin got a trailer, installed a bathtub for thirteen-foot-long alligator Cannibal Jake, and toured the Jersey shore or worked with Masonic lodges to set up in towns where people would pay a dime each to see Jake. The park was renamed Gatorland in 1954. In 1962, Godwin's youngest son, Frank, designed a walk-through gator jaw for the entrance. One of the most memorable attractions was added in 1983—the Gator Jumparoo, where the hungry reptiles lunge for chicken meat suspended on a wire. Today, Gatorland covers 110 acres, and the road Godwin chose fared pretty well too, now home to Walt Disney World, Universal Studios, and Sea World.

The distinctive gator jaw entrance has a somewhat similar twin to the east at Jungle Adventures, formerly known as Gator Jungle. When 200-foot-long Swampy was built in 1992, a legal challenge led to some changes, but the world's largest gator still houses the gift shop, offices, and ticket counter to the twenty-acre park and wildlife sanctuary for such animals as hybrid panther-cougars. Swampy is aptly named, for the park is set in a swamp. The park offers tours and shows, a boat ride through an alligator-inhabited swamp, and a Native American Village. There are 200 gators in the park, as well as an estimated 10,000 being grown for meat and skin.

The St. Augustine Alligator Farm (and now Zoological Park) is the granddaddy of roadside gator parks. A couple men began collecting alli-

Swampy the Giant holds the admission counter, gift shop, and offices of Jungle Adventures in Christmas, Florida. Built in 1992, Swampy is 200 feet, 1 inch long. SHARI PAGLIA

gators on Anastasia Island in the 1880s and displayed them at South Beach, a destination for tourists on the South Beach Railway Company's island tram. In the 1920s, the owners moved closer to downtown St. Augustine, eventually acquiring animals from other zoos. The park has grown to more than 1,000 crocs and gators and features all twenty-three species of crocodilians in individual habitats, the only such facility in the world. The star is Maximo, hatched in Australia in 1971 and grown to more than fifteen feet and 1,250 pounds.

Though Florida predominates, the rest of the country has its share of animal attractions. Competing for the gator market is Alligator Adventure in North Myrtle Beach. This attraction, which bills itself as the "reptile capital of the world," also has the ever-popular gator jumping for food. Jungle Adventures in Virginia features a variety of wildlife, with lots of reptiles, but the focus is on mountain lions and other big cats, not tropical animals. In Gatlinburg, the Three Bears Gift Shop is one of the few old-time roadside attractions where the emphasis has not yet shifted to education, but rather just the novelty of seeing

You'll find five bears at the Three Bears Gift Shop in Pigeon Forge, Tennessee.

Way up in the sublime White Mountains of New Hampshire on Route 3, just south of where the Old Man in the Mountain used to hold forth, is one of the great remaining roadside attractions in America. Clark's Trading Post began as a sled dog ranch in the late 1920s. Today the sled dogs are long gone, but the Clark family still holds forth with energy and enthusiasm. The major drawing card now is the best darned trained bear show this side of Moscow. These talented beasts can ride scooters, slam-dunk basketballs, and perform other stupendous feats. But that's not all that's going on here. There's also a steam locomotive ride, an "old main street," a tilted-floor mystery house, and a great gift shop offering a wide variety of merchandise—stuff we'd love to take home, like moccasins and fine clothes, as well as souvenirs and trinkets to remind us and our friends of good times and a great place. This fourth-generation family business is ingenious, inventive, and more fun than a barrel full of bears, which indeed seem to have a great time rolling around in barrels and eating ice cream treats out of the bungholes.

—JOHN MARGOLIES, author of *Fun along the Road: American Roadside Attractions*

Pemigewasset rides his scooter with trainer Maureen Clark at Clark's Trading Post in North Woodstock, New Hampshire. LISA ZIMMER CLARK

bears in captivity—in this case, five of them. At Clark's Trading Post in New Hampshire, Maureen Clark not only trains and cares for performing bears, but she says she loves them too. The attraction also includes Merlin's Mystical Mansion, a two-and-a-half-mile steam train ride, and the acrobatics of the Seyranyan Family Circus, but it's the bear shows that are best remembered. Murray Clark has worked with bears for more than sixty years and, like his daughter, has a great affection for them. The bears are not muzzled or leashed and seem to enjoy the shows as much as the audience.

An attraction that features no animals, but can only be described as animal-themed, is the arch across the main street of Afton, Wyoming. The World's Largest Elkhorn Arch spans seventy-five feet of four-lane U.S. 89. Elk shed their horns annually, and folks collect and sell them for decorations. The arch in Afton is made of 3,011 such antlers and weighs fifteen tons.

Neither will you find animals to pet at the Rancho La Brea Tar Pits, in the heart of Los Angeles, though the site has attracted living things for 30,000 years. That's the problem—the asphaltic sand is so sticky, it's been trapping and killing animals since the ice age, such as the saber-toothed cats and mammoths that once roamed the region. More than a million bones have been recovered from 231 species of vertebrates since excavations began in 1906. About ten gallons of the sticky substance still bubbles to the surface every day, continuing to trap everything from birds to dogs to humans. Nearby Hancock Park features life-size replicas of several extinct mammals, including an elephant family struggling to get Mom unstuck. The Page Museum, a satellite of the Natural History Museum of Los Angeles County, has the world's largest collection of extinct ice age plants and animals.

Replica animals are perhaps more common than real ones along the roadside. The Jackalope started as a joke when a couple hunters who also knew taxidermy mounted deer antlers on a jackrabbit. For decades, while the myth of the hybrid animal grew, jackalope souvenirs became one of the staples of their hometown of Douglas, Wyoming. The Chamber of Commerce has issued

The Rancho La Brea Tar Pits in the heart of Los Angeles features this re-created animal emergency.

Trees of Mystery near Klamath, California, is the only roadside attraction I know that truly sells immortality. Oh, you can't take it home with you. But you can feel it if you linger long enough under the redwood towers. I've watched people waltz in front of the Cathedral Tree. A pixie moment. A pirouette. One snapshot of a lifetime. When I saw that, I was left to wonder. Do trees have memories? If they do, they'll remember me and tell someone someday that I passed through.

—THOMAS REPP, executive editor, *American Road* magazine

Beverly and John Greer (Thomas's mom and stepdad) clowning around at Trees of Mystery in Klamath, Callifornia. THOMAS REPP

Andrew and Jenny Wood and daughter Vienna visit Arches National Park, Utah.

thousands of jackalope hunting licenses and helped erect a statue of the animal. The original sat in the median of Center Street until it was run down by a truck. A newer, bigger one was erected in Jackalope Square in 1987.

Affection has likewise grown around a giant blue termite in Rhode Island. Nibbles Woodaway welcomes drivers to Providence from the roof of New England Pest Control. The big bug is so popular that the state even used his image on a lottery ticket—until a competitor complained, but by then, the game was over.

Natural wonders are among the oldest attractions and continue to mesmerize. Some, like the rock formations in Utah's Arches National Park, are unique enough to be considered roadside attractions, though you'll find no wacky souvenir stands inside this park. Other wonders have been turned into tourist traps, to the consternation of some and the pleasure of many. Not far from Arches, south of Moab, Utah, are a gift shop, trading post, statuary and cactus garden, and most notably, a furnished underground home. Hole N' The Rock has fourteen rooms covering 5,000 square feet, supported by pillars of rock. It was built by Albert and Gladys Christensen, with Albert excavating 50,000 cubic feet of sandstone over twelve years. After his death in

FAN FAVORITE

Constructed of marble slabs from a Gold Rush-era cemetery, San Francisco's Wave Organ looks like an ancient temple perched on the end of a spit of land near the Golden Gate Yacht Club. We might never have known about it if we hadn't been invited to visit by the Wave Organ's creator, Peter Richards. Advising us to arrive before daybreak when the tide was high, he showed us how to listen to the bay through long tubes that descend into the water. We've been back to the Wave Organ many times since, but nothing will ever compare with watching the sun come up over the Golden Gate while listening to the haunting music of the ocean that first time.

—MEGAN EDWARDS, founding editor of www.RoadTripAmerica.com

The Wave Organ in San Francisco Bay. MEGAN EDWARDS

Three-and-a-half-year-old Dee Dee Groves Porter with her family and their new 1950 Ford at Yosemite National Park. This was in late spring or summer 1951, as they were moving from Texas to California. Note her brothers' matching Hopalong Cassidy T-shirts. DOROTHY DELINA PORTER

1957, Gladys continued the work until her passing in 1974. They're laid to rest in a small rock cove near the home.

Among the most popular "live" natural attractions are the giant redwood trees of California, many preserved in the state and national parks. Perhaps best known are the trees whose trunks have been carved out for cars to drive through for a fee. Along the Avenue of the Trees in the northern part of the state, the privately owned Tour-Thru Tree is about 725 years old, its tunnel cut in 1976. The opening is more than seven feet wide and nine-and-a-half-feet high. Also famous and the subject of many a postcard is the Redwood Tree Service Station, now a mini-museum, and the thirty-two-foot long One-Log House, made from a tree 2,100 years old. It was built on wheels

to be mobile, and though it never toured the country, it's had to move numerous times. A sign of changing times is that it's now called the One-Log House Espresso and Gifts. A good way to learn more about the big trees is at Trees of Mystery. A walking trail takes you past numerous unusual tree formations, and six-pasenger aerial gondolas take riders through the Redwood Forest canopy. Out front, giant statues of famed lumberman Paul Bunyan (forty-nine feet, two inches tall) and his blue ox, Babe, greet visitors.

The only other flora to hit the roadside big time is the saguaro (suh-WAR-oh) cactus, recognizable by its arms that make it somewhat humanlike. They're popular in westerns, whether appropriate or not, to give an "authentic" American West look. They also appear on signs across the country, but in reality, the saguaro is mostly found in south-western Arizona. Douglas Towne, who has written about the phenomenon of the "wandering saguaro," says motels and Mexican restaurants readily adopted them starting in the late 1930s to evoke the mythology of the West.

A saguaro cactus at a sort of Wild West Corral in Oatman, Arizona, wraps itself around road-tripper Douglas Towne, who has written about the phenomenon of the "wandering saguaro" as seen in signage across the country. LIZ BOETTCHER

Tunnel Rock, California. CHRIS EPTING

Perhaps the ultimate melding of nature and roadside hucksterism are "gravity hill" attractions, which qualify as wonders or hokum, depending on your stance. The operators and tour guides attribute the logic-defying happenings to an upheaval that shifted gravity's pull, a strong outcropping of magnetic rock, or even objects buried by aliens. Anyone whose been through them, with the same stunts repeated across the country, will recognize the house, or "mystery shack," that is so tilted that water flows and balls roll uphill, chairs will hang from a wall, and a person grasping an overhead door frame can't hang straight down. Another standard illusion is having two people stand back-to-back, and when they switch positions, their heights are different—at least, that's how it looks on old postcards. Compasses are said to go haywire, and birds and animals reportedly avoid these areas.

The oldest of these is the Oregon Vortex and House of Mystery, opened in 1930. The house reportedly was built in 1904 as a gold-mining company office and toolshed. After the mine closed, it is said to have slid off its foundation—a standard mystery hill storyline—and then Scottish immigrant John Litster, a geologist and physicist, opened it to the public. A decade later, the Mystery Spot opened to the south in Santa Cruz. This site has been visited by psychologists from the University of California in Berkeley, who concluded that the illusion comes from the human need to estab-

FAN FAVORITE

In the summer of 1985, my parents and I took a weeklong road trip to the Upper Peninsula of Michigan, Wisconsin, and Minnesota. On the third day, we found ourselves in Copper Harbor, Michigan. One of the locals told us we had to check out the local dump at dusk when the bears came out of the woods to have their dinner. Out of curiosity, we got directions and made our way there. Upon arriving, we found a scene out of *The Great Outdoors*, with about fifteen other cars whose occupants were tossing all sorts of junk food, and even trash, in the direction of a dozen or so black bears. The EPA closed the dump in the early 1990s, and the bears returned to the woods for a much healthier diet of leaves and berries.

—PAT BREMER, American Road web board moderator

Mystery Hill in the Irish Hills of southern Michigan.

A scary—or scared—tree at the Mystery Hill in Marblehead, Ohio.

lish horizontal and vertical orientations and the
way we take our cues from the immediate context
if we can't see the horizon. But don't let science or
logic spoil the fun at these places.

In 1949, George Hudson was inspired by the
above two attractions to find his own mystery
spot, Confusion Hill in Willow Creek, California.
He believed there were many places where gravity and magnetism joined forces in strange ways,
so he built the Gravity House here to enhance the
phenomenon. Just as popular with kids is the
Redwood Shoehouse, used as a float in a parade
in 1947 and here ever since opening. The site also
has a Mountain Train Ride that climbs one and a
quarter miles by following a switchback pattern
uphill through old-growth redwoods to a display

Members of Darkride and Funhouse Enthusiasts (DAFE) meet every year at a different park. In 2003, it was Big Mike's
in Cave City, Kentucky. Here DAFE cofounder Rick Davis is trying to figure out this ill-proportioned room with members Marina Faupel, left, and Jasminne Grimm at right. RICK DAVIS

Of all the roadside attractions I've visited in my life, caves enchant me as much today as when I was a little kid peering out the back window on a long family trip. Caves are not randomly distributed along the roadside, but associated with limestone environments known as karst landscapes. Groundwater charged with carbon dioxide eats away the calcium carbonate in the limestone to create the cavity, and then subsequent water seeping into the cave redeposits the calcite in all sorts of weird and wonderful ways.

Show caves can't be relocated to places with better market potential. They are where nature put them and interpreted for the public in whatever scientific or quirky way the proprietor deems fit. Though the geological processes are similar, every show cave is different. Smoke Hole Caverns in West Virginia and Iowa's Spook Cave have something to offer that can't be found even in great caves of the National Park System, such as Mammoth or Carlsbad.

At the entrance, time-worn legends are recited—tragic tales of star-crossed Indian lovers, robbers' loot, or hermits, historical facts optional. Inside, show caves represent multiple generations of human interpretation reflected in the names given the formations. Romantic cave tours of the nineteenth and early twentieth centuries stressed Indian legends, the Classics, and Christian references. After World War II, pop culture icons and formation fables entertained Baby Boomer children with rocky versions of comic strip characters. The current trend toward cave science presented by a generation of proprietors with degrees in geology and biology (as well as business) leaves many of the old imagination formations to go unreferenced by the guides. Regardless of the method of interpretation, at some point along the tour it's "lights out" for the creepy sensation of "total darkness."

No show cave would be complete without a good gift shop hawking postcards, floaty pens, slingshots, and rubber-tipped spears, all stamped with the cave's name. The pennant my parents bought me on my boyhood trip to Lincoln Caverns has faded, the keychain lost long ago, but that fascinating hole is still in the ground, and the memories stored from my adventure there will be replicated by my children, making true the inevitability that cave tourists breed more cave tourists.

—KEVIN PATRICK, author of *Pennsylvania Caves and Other Rocky Roadside Wonders*

Caves across the continent have drawn tourists for more than a century. Onondaga, Bridal, and Meramec are all in Missouri.

The Blue Whale of Catoosa, Oklahoma, captured my heart while my husband was writing his book, *Route 66: The Empires of Amusement*. It did so because it was love that spawned this magnificent attraction. The whale's builder, Hugh, designed, built, and gave the whale to Zelta, his beloved. Hugh knew Zelta cared for all the creatures that walk the earth and he wanted to give her the biggest as a demonstration of his devotion to her. Zelta and Hugh are both gone, but thankfully their family stills owns the awesome creation. As long as the whale stands, I know that love can endure the test of time, albeit in the form of a big, smiling, blue whale.

—BECKY REPP, coordinating editor of *American Road* magazine

The Blue Whale in Catoosa, Oklahoma, once again welcomes travelers to an oasis from the busy highway.

of old logging equipment. But it's the sign that draws tourists to what is now Campbell Brothers Confusion Hill: "Home of the Rare, Elusive CHIPALOPE," which is, of course, a chipmunk with antlers.

On the other side of the country, a couple Mystery Hill sites are not far from each other, one in Ohio along Lake Erie and the other in the Irish Hills of Michigan. In Ohio, visitors get twice the entertainment—gravity-defying house and Prehistoric Forest. When we stopped at the Ohio one a decade ago, guests visited the dinos by tram car and shot at them with machine guns. On our recent return trip, bored tour guides led us through the house, then left us to walk the dino trail alone, the tram retired years ago. In Kentucky, not far from Wigwam Village, Big Mike's Rock and Gift Shop and Mystery House advertises that it's the state's largest rock shop, but it also has a tilted, gravity-defying house.

Other, noncommercial sites are experienced by driving your car to a spot and observing the vehicle appear to get pulled uphill. The illusion is often created by a hill or rock strata looking higher relative to the surrounding landscape. The best known of these is Spook Hill in Lake Wells, Florida. It's easy to find; just look for the nearby Spook Hill Elementary School. Old postcards for it that picture a ghost are matched in zaniness by the modern brochure for Gravity Hill near Bedford, Pennsylvania. The folks promoting this site have a lot of fun and offer some practical tips, too. Even if you're a nonbeliever, it's hard to resist their reasons for visiting, such as, "The wonder bra works better than advertised" and that it's "the last place the cops would think to look for you."

SPOTLIGHT ON
Dinosaurs

Dinosaurs have enjoyed their role as leading roadside attractions since the 1930s. One of the first was a twenty-five-foot-long concrete critter in the Badlands of South Dakota, built by a general-store owner in the tiny town of Creston to catch tourists on their way to Mount Rushmore, then being carved. Rapid City, even closer to the mountainside presidents, was bitten by the dino bug too and made its Dinosaur Park a federal relief project. Five giant concrete dinosaurs still overlook the city and a gift shop, which has two mini-dinos of its own.

Far to the east in Michigan, Paul and Lora Domke were building their own interpretation of dinos on forty acres of drained swampland. Opened in the late 1930s, Dinosaur Gardens mixes the big creatures with other prehistoric animals, cavemen and cavewomen, and Christian imagery. A statue of Jesus holding a globe greets visitors at the entrance, and the staircase into an apatosaurus (brontosaurus to old-timers) leads to a display with Jesus as "The Greatest Heart."

Dino parks embracing religion have gained ground in recent years. One of the best-known sites is Cabazon Dinosaurs in California, where displays explain that dinosaurs were born at the time of creation some 6,000 years ago. An August 27, 2005, *L.A. Times* article says there are "at least half a dozen other roadside attractions nationwide that use the giant reptiles' popularity in seeking to win converts to creationism. And more are

The T-rex in Cabazon, California, looks to be chasing a bird for lunch. RICK SEBAK

on the way. As one advocate said, 'We're putting evolutionists on notice: We're taking the dinosaurs back.'" The Cabazon attraction was started in 1964 by Claude Bell, who was then seventy-three. He had grown up in the shadow of Lucy the giant elephant in Margate, New Jersey, and had crafted displays for Knott's Berry Farm. His 150-foot-long brontosaurus and 65-foot-tall tyrannosaurus are perhaps best known for their appearance in the 1985 film, *Pee-Wee's Big Adventure*.

The two dozen "scientifically correct" creatures at Prehistoric Forest in Oregon were built over four decades by sculptor E. V. Nelson, all in a lush primeval-looking rain forest. This is quite a contrast to the Prehistoric Forests in the East, where more folksy dinos are set in the leafy woods. A newer pair of attractions, the Dinosaur Worlds in Kentucky and Florida, emphasize activities and education while still filling their sites with what kids love best—big dinos, more than 100 in Kentucky and 150 in Florida.

Escape from Dinosaur Kingdom in Natural Bridge, Virginia, is master artist Mark Cline's homage to two

Visitors will find "the Heart of Jesus" inside this giant dino at Dinosaur Gardens in Ossineke, Michigan. DEBRA JANE SELTZER

Joe and Kori Paull visit Cline's dino place in Natural Bridge, Virginia, with Robbie and Sophie.

A giant jaw greets visitors to Dinosaur Land in northern Virginia.

historical favorites, dinosaurs and Civil War soldiers. He's also crafted figures for other sites, including the somewhat nearby Dinosaur Land, which has perhaps twenty of them. Joanne Leight says Cline's creations are much more realistic than the originals from 1963, when her dad founded the park. Early postcards show the crossroads attraction as the Rebel Korn'r Gift Shop, with a couple dinos out front. Part of the fun these days is finding the out-of-place creatures among the dozens of fiberglass animals, such as a giant cobra, a thirteen-foot-tall praying mantis, a thirty-foot-tall King Kong, and a sixty-foot-long shark. The best part—whether you're a kid or an overgrown kid—is the gift shop that visitors must pass through when entering or leaving the attraction. It's filled with all those things you wish your parents had bought you, and now's your chance to get them.

CHAPTER 5

FUN FOOD

Ron Aigner and Diane Wiescamp and their restoration project, the former Coney Island hot-dog stand. In 2006, they moved it to Bailey, Colorado, where they hope to make it part of a larger road-side food and lodging attraction.

When it comes to food options, perhaps only Denver offers a choice between a silly time at a mock Mexican resort and a painstakingly re-created frontier fort.

Casa Bonita sits in a strip mall but is easy to spot by its eighty-five-foot-high pink tower and fountain out front. Customers enter and follow a line to order fare that is pretty streamlined: all-you-can-eat beef or chicken dinners, which roll through a little door to your tray. But you don't go there for the cuisine; you go for the strolling mariachis, the gunfights and magicians, the game room and gift shop. Tables are scattered throughout the dimly lit 52,000 square feet, but all have a view of a thirty-foot waterfall where cliff divers and others perform. Kids like to explore the palm-filled interior and crawl-through cave.

The Fort, on the other hand, is where presidents and world leaders dine when in Denver. The Fort is a living replica of Bent's Fort, Colorado's first trading post, from 1833 to 1849. The original, on the Santa Fe Trail, was a trading center for the many nationalities and native tribes. The re-creation was the idea of Sam Arnold, who chanced upon a drawing of the fort in 1962 and thought the design would make an interesting

The Fort in Morrison, Colorado, is a painstaking reproduction of Bent's Fort, which served traders and travelers along the Santa Fe Trail.

home. When banks refused to lend money for such a house, he added a restaurant to the plan. A twenty-five-man crew from Taos made 80,000 forty-five-pound adobe bricks on-site and hewed the supporting beams. Nine dining rooms surround a central courtyard. The St. Vrain Bar floor was made with the traditional mixture of earth and ox blood but covered with wood planks to make it walkable. There's also a museum and great bookstore. Sam and daughter Holly Arnold Kinney created The Tesoro Foundation in 1999 to protect and share the region's artistic and cultural treasures. The foundation sponsors cultural events, reenactments, and an annual lecture series. The menu includes authentic dishes like elk, quail, and bison marrow bones. Don't let bison eggs confuse you—they're pickled quail eggs wrapped in buffalo sausage and served with raspberry-jalapeño jam. As for buffalo steaks, The Fort sells more than any other independently owned restaurant in the country. Sam passed away in June 2006, but his memorial service carried on the traditions he was so fond of. Two months later, his beloved site was listed in the National Register of Historic Places.

Neither re-created forts nor Mexican resorts have caught on widely, but other themed restau-

A western comedy routine plays out above the waterfall at Casa Bonita in Denver.

One of my favorite places growing up in the 1960s and 1970s was a little section of Oxnard, California, transected by railroad tracks and U.S. 101. From the highway, you could see a giant neon sign announcing "Wagon Wheel Junction" over an animated, spinning wagon wheel. Wagon Wheel Bowl, still there with its original bowling pin sign, and a Putt-Putt Golf, now gone, were side-by-side entertainment options.

Just down the block was the Roller Gardens, a pre-disco roller rink with palm trees and flashing lights. This was the junior high school hangout where parents dropped off their kids for the day. The place is still there, but updated and renamed Pacific View Inline Hockey.

At night, sometimes my parents took me to the El Ranchito Restaurant, which had a rustic interior and served huge portions. We never ate at the Wagon Wheel Restaurant, but I always loved staring at the sign. Both restaurants and the sign are still there.

My favorite place to eat was the Trade Winds Restaurant, unforgivably demolished. I didn't care much for the food but I loved the A-frame architecture and tiki decor. A koi fish pond under a little bridge leading to the entrance set the mood. It was a Polynesian palace with bamboo, fountains, and gigantic tropical fish tanks. There were singers, hula girls, and spellbinding floor shows with fire dancers. My favorite part of the experience was drinking from hollowed-out pineapples.

—DEBRA JANE SELTZER, www.roadsidenut.com

The Trade Winds tiki restaurant in Oxnard, California, now demolished. TIM HAACK

rants have always prospered. Though far fewer today, tiki restaurants were the rage after World War II. Devotees track the survivors in books and online forums. The originator of the trend was Ernest Gantt, who opened a tiny bar in Hollywood just after Prohibition ended. He called it Beachcomber's and specialized in rum drinks, most famously the Mai Tai. When he moved across the street, Gantt expanded into tropical-themed food and changed the name to Don the Beachcomber, as friends familiar with his bootlegging background had taken to calling him Don. His place set the standard for Polynesian-style restaurants, though the food was mostly Cantonese-style Chinese served with flair. After World War II, he moved to Honolulu, Hawaii, where he opened another location while developing the area around it as the International Marketplace. His office was in the limbs of a giant banyan tree in the middle of the market. Gantt's chain of restaurants spread across California and then the United States, inspiring competitors such as Trader Vic's. As the Polynesian fad waned, so did the chain, but a couple new Don the Beachcombers have recently opened as the style is again becoming popular for restaurants and even more noticeably at water parks.

A number of surviving tiki nightspots are time capsules. Like all the great venues, the Kon Tiki Restaurant and Lounge in Tucson, Arizona, is guarded out front by giant tiki torches, and inside are all the necessary Polynesian touches. In San Francisco, the Tonga Room features a swimming pool turned lagoon in the middle of the restaurant. Every half hour, a thunderstorm of water, sound, and light refills the pond. The Mai-Kai Restaurant in Fort Lauderdale, run by the same family since opening in 1956, has all the usual tropical touches and artifacts, as well as outdoor gardens and a dazzling forty-five-minute revue performed twice nightly by native Polynesian dancers.

On a country road in Portland, Connecticut, not far from where I live, I came upon a huge wiener on wheels, resting in a gigantic bun, complete with mustard and relish—all made out of molded plastic. It was the Top Dog mobile hot-dog stand, calling out to me by the roadside. I thought, "Claes Oldenburg, eat your heart out!" Not only was it a humorous statement about scale and juxtaposition, but it served the best chili dog in New England. Art, surrealism, and fine dining, all in one parking lot!

—BILL GRIFFITH, cartoonist, Zippy the Pinhead

Zippy visits the "Top Dog" in Portland, Oregon. BILL GRIFFITH

Along the same line, but more rustic, is Clifton's Cafeteria in Los Angeles. Clifford Clinton opened a South Seas–themed eatery in 1931. Four years later, he purchased a nondescript cafeteria and transformed it into a lush wonderland, putting a stream through the dining room that was fed by a twenty-foot waterfall. Posts were transformed into tree and sculpted rocks were placed throughout the restaurant. The cafeteria at one time featured singing waiters and live organ music. Other locations opened, but these have now closed, leaving only the original, known as Clifton's Brookdale. A wide variety of food is made from scratch.

Many offbeat restaurants were built between the world wars. The era marked the height of pro-

This pig-shaped stand in San Antonio, Texas, twelve feet tall and ten feet long, sits next to a Pig Stand restaurant on Presa Street in San Antonio. DEBRA JANE SELTZER

grammatic architecture, where buildings conveyed what they sold. The Big Duck on Long Island sold duck eggs. In Bedford, Pennsylvania, a giant coffeepot used to be a café. It is now restored but no longer sells food. In Ipswich, Massachusetts, the Clam Box looks like a big cardboard carry-out container. Sometimes the design was simply whimsical, such as in Natchez, Mississippi, where Mammy's Cupboard is a café inside a brick-skirted, twenty-eight foot-tall black woman. She was built in 1940 to appeal to tourists in town to see the town's antebellum mansions. Today, such caricatures can be seen as offensive, but they are also looked upon as interesting historical artifacts and local landmarks. Los Angeles was the pinnacle of programmatic buildings, taking the shapes of boats, airplanes, windmills, barrels, oranges, tepees, owls, and jails. Best known are the hat-shaped Brown Derby restaurants.

In San Antonio, Texas, a Big Pig building reportedly housed a restaurant selling pork sandwiches. Stories abound as to the origins of the Big Pig. Some people think it is the one seen in an old photo of a drive-up stand in Harlingen, Texas, but

Programmatic buildings like this igloo-shaped stand in Toledo, Ohio, often help convey what's sold inside, in this case ice cream. Orders are placed and picked up through the windows. Picnic tables are similarly round. DEBRA JANE SELTZER

a comparison of the two, especially the ears, shows they are not the same. Another story is that it was a barbecue stand and later a house and bordello, though there's little room inside for liv-

---

It was amazing how little square footage was needed to conduct a seasonal business in the 1950s. My favorite survivor from that period is Mountain Mist, a little ice cream stand along Route 86, the main road leading into the Adirondack village of Saranac Lake,

New York. What makes Mountain Mist endearing is its combination of modesty and period stylistic flourishes. The small, simple building has a canted front wall of glass that lets you see right into the interior and a tilted roof rising toward the passing parade of motorists. Keep the overhang painted white and it remains a postwar classic.

—PHILIP LANGDON, author of *Orange Roofs, Golden Arches: The Architecture of American Chain Restaurants* and senior editor of *New Urban News*

FAN FAVORITE

Mountain Mist Ice Cream (originally Custard) in Saranac Lake, New York. Architectural writer Philip Langdon says many drive-in and drive-up stands in the 1940s and 1950s featured large, canted windows to attract passing motorists while deflecting the glare of customers' headlights. PHILIP LANGDON

We were starving, needing a rest stop, when suddenly Bozo's Hot Pit Bar-B-Que in Mason, Tennessee, came into view. The barbecue sandwich was delicious, the best I had ever eaten in a region known for barbecue. Added treats for an architectural historian were photos of Bozo's earlier buildings and a brochure with the business's history, including a 1980s trademark lawsuit with Bozo the Clown.

Just to be sure it was not my starvation that made me think the food was great, I have gone back often. It's still good and served fast. The only problem is deciding whether you want fries or onion rings on the side. If Bozo's is closed, Gus's World Famous Fried Chicken is down the road, but that's another story.

—CLAUDETTE STAGER, National Register,
Tennessee Historical Commission, Nashville,
and coeditor of *Looking beyond the Highway:
Dixie Roads and Culture*

Bozo's 1950 building and 1989 neon sign welcome diners in western Tennessee. Named for founder Thomas Jefferson "Bozo" Williams, the business spent nine years wrangling with the holder of the more famous Bozo trademark but prevailed.

ing or hanky-panky. Most believe the Big Pig was a carhop shelter at a Pig Stand drive-in (considered the first drive-in restaurant chain) on Broadway in San Antonio, and then ended up in the parking lot of a bar on South Roosevelt. By the 1990s, it had to move again, and locals got permission from the Pig Stand chain to move it to the current location on South Presa Street, where it houses a lone table for two. Pig Stands became famous for their "pig sandwiches" and grew to 120 locations but later dwindled to about half a dozen. In 2005, the Texas Pig Stands chain filed for bankruptcy, and in November 2006, it was forced to close, to the dismay of longtime employees and customers. The Van's Pig Stands chain in Oklahoma has fared better. Its Shawnee store, opened in 1930 and relocated in 1935, is the state's oldest barbecue restaurant owned and operated by the same family. The Norman location opened in 1994 in a rehabbed 1920s Spanish Revival gas station.

Preservation is particularly difficult for roadside businesses, which must serve the public's changing tastes. Near Oxnard, California, the Trade Winds Restaurant was torn down in the 1980s and is now an RV sales lot, the El Ranchito is closed and set to be demolished, and the Wagon Wheel Restaurant, also closed, is considered one of the best remaining examples of midcentury roadside architecture in Ventura County. Martin Smith, the leading figure in Oxnard's twentieth-century growth, built the restaurant and motel in 1947. A slaughterhouse formerly at the site inspired him to apply a western theme, with help from a Hollywood designer. He used old army barracks from the nearby Seabee Base for motel units. A big sign featured a horse-drawn wagon. The landowners have proposed housing and retail stores on the site, but the county's Cultural Heritage Board wants to work with the city council to designate parts of the building as landmarks. Officials even think it could be eligible for listing in the National Register, not only as an important example of roadside architecture, but also for being one of the first projects by Smith. As of early 2007, demolition was imminent.

It's been more that thirty years since I first crossed the Mississippi River at Memphis and saw the Arkansas Delta. The seemingly endless fields of rich, dark earth stood in stark contrast to the stony, glacial till that passed for topsoil in the Catskill Mountains where I was born and raised.

After an hour or two of driving through lush fields of rice, cotton, and soybeans, I crossed the White River at DeValls Bluff and stopped for lunch at Craig's Bar-B-Q. The building wasn't much by modern standards, but the parking lot was busy. Inside were half a dozen kitchen tables and assorted chairs that might have come from the Ralph and Alice Kramden collection. I have since come to realize that this is a good sign when looking for authentic southern barbecue.

Craig's smoked meat, tangy red sauce, slow-cooked beans, and slaw were enough to make me forsake my northern home, but best of all was the pie. I finished my meal with a slice of chocolate cream the size of a steam iron and as dark and rich as delta soil. It might well have been the best thing I ever put in my mouth.

Craig's was opened by Lawrence Craig in 1947 and is still in the same location on the south side of Route 70, just west of downtown DeValls Bluff. The lady who makes the pies has a small block building in a backyard across the road. It's named the Family Pie Shop, but locals just call it Mary's.

—DAVID MALCOLM ROSE, photorealistic modeler of roadside architecture, www.davidmalcolmrose.com

Aiden and Angela Rose visit the Pie Shop, which was opened by Mary Thomas in 1977 in a former bike shed.
DAVID MALCOLM ROSE

Sometimes the architecture and food combine for an unforgettable experience. At the nine locations of The Medieval Times Dinner and Tournament, guests dine around a giant oval arena where eleventh-century knights perform. Visitor get colored crowns to match their seating areas and the knights they'll cheer. Then "serving wenches" and "serfs" deliver the four-course meal of soup, chicken, spare ribs, and pastry, with no silverware but plenty of napkins. Meanwhile, the princess and her suitors perform, leading to a battle between six knights in games of skill to prove their valor, and then a joust using ten-foot lances. Once they are unseated, they continue their noisy clash with sword, ax, mace, and bola. The first location opened in Spain in 1973, and the first in the United States at Kissimmee, Florida, in 1983. It is rather pricey for a family, but joining the Loyalty Club earns regular customers discounts.

Even seemingly simple foods can inspire devotion. At Del's, it's the frozen lemonade in paper cups that attracts the faithful. The company traces the recipe to 1840, when Franco DeLucia in Naples, Italy, would store snow in the caves and then combine it with sugar and locally grown lemons come summer. His son Angelo devised a machine to make it consistently and opened the first Del's stand in 1948. The stands and mobile units are found mostly across Rhode Island, though they've spread as far as California and the Virgin Islands. At Red's Eats in Wiscasset, Maine, the menus are as small as the roadside stand, with burgers and fries, but it's the seafood that folks come for: clams, shrimp, scallops, and especially the lobster rolls, which many claim are the best anywhere. They're not cheap but are made from about a pound of lobster in a toasted bun. Another favorite is the hot dog, split and filled with either

On the west side of U.S. 11 just north of Harrison-burg, Virginia, stands the Bar-B-Q Ranch drive-in restaurant. This interesting relic of the drive-in era features "Good Food . . . Quick Service" with a dining room, curb service, take-out, and catering. The pork barbecue sandwiches, served on warm buns with cole slaw on the side, are excellent, as are the hamburgers and french fries. The pie is a first-rate dessert, and the milkshakes are outstanding—the kind I remember from the postwar years when drive-ins were at their peak. The Bar-B-Q Ranch is well worth a detour as you pass by on I-81.

—ARCHIE LOSS, author of *Pop Dreams: Music, Movies, and the Media in the 1960s*

Owner Faye Bland has run the Bar-B-Q Ranch drive-in in Harrisonburg, Virginia, for more than twenty years and bottles her own sauce. The place opened fifty-two years ago.

Red's Eats in Wiscasset, Maine, is famous for its lobster rolls. RICK SEBAK

cheese or bacon, then battered and deep-fried. The shack opened in Boothbay in 1938, then moved to Wiscasset in 1954. Powers Hamburgers in Fort Wayne, Indiana, was founded in 1940 as part of a chain started in Michigan that was similar to White Castle, with tiny, tidy buildings where customers buy bagfuls of small burgers topped with fried onions.

Louis' Lunch in New Haven, Connecticut, claims to be where the first hamburger sandwich was served in 1900, although many other places make the same claim. The story goes that when someone asked for a quick meal at his lunch wagon, owner Louis Lassen broiled a beef patty and put it between two slices of bread. Louis's

Powers Hamburgers in Fort Wayne, Indiana, looks a
lot like contemporary White Tower and White Castle
restaurants, all famed for their small, inexpensive
burgers with onions.

grandson Ken carries on the family tradition of
hamburgers broiled vertically in the original cast-
iron grill, served between two slices of toast, with
cheese, tomato, and onion the only acceptable
garnish. Another place known for burgers is the
XXX restaurant in West Lafayette, Indiana,
where four patties fill buns as big as a plate. The
XXX chain of stands was started as a way to hawk
XXX-brand soft drinks in the 1920s. Nearby Pur-
due University students might favor the Duane
Purvis All-American burger, which is topped with
peanut butter. The stand has been here since
1929. Jack and Ruth Ehresman bought it in 1980,
and their son Greg and wife, Carrie, took over in
1999. They're proud of the 100 percent unfrozen
sirloin they use, and in fact, Jack still comes in to
cut the meat every morning.

At the Old Spanish Sugar Mill Grill and Griddle House near DeLeon Springs, Florida, you
cook your own breakfast. A waitress brings the
basics, then you make eggs, pancakes, or french
toast on a grill at the center of your table. No
checks either—just tell the cashier what you had.

The tradition started with the owner Patricia
Schwarz's father, a fifth-generation gristmiller, at
a bakery he ran in New York City.

For a bigger meal, the Cattlemen's Steakhouse
has changed little through the decades, which is
just how they like things here. It opened in 1910,
when endless streams of cattle were being driven
to Oklahoma City. That year, the first packing-
house opened in this area, which became known
as Stockyards City. The stockyards boomed, creating thousands of jobs in the slaughter industry.
By 1961, however, the packing plants had closed
rather than update. Today a Main Street program
maintains the old flavor of the town's seventy-five
businesses, including western wear and the headquarters for the International Professional Rodeo
Association, and the adjacent Oklahoma National
Stockyards are the world's largest stocker and
feeder cattle markets. The steakhouse menu
offers many cuts, including strip sirloin, rib eye,
and the Presidential Choice T-bone, what President Bush ate when he dined here.

One of the most popular style of eateries is the
drive-in restaurant, which offers the greatest variety and survival rate of classic signs. Drive-ins

Signs for the Cattlemen's Steakhouse and Café in
Oklahoma City are joined by the vintage neon for
National Saddlery.

The Vista Drive-In was founded in 1964 by Charles and Martha Streeter in Manhattan, Kansas. It and three other locations are now run by son Brad and his wife, Karen, and two of their three sons.

predominated in the 1950s and 1960s, but most closed or converted to sit-down restaurants by the 1970s. Groupings of drive-ins continue to prosper in a few areas, such as southern Michigan, where the Chick-Inn is one of many interesting finds. The sign is not fancy, though its "time to eat" clock is charming. Rather, it's the zigzag neon along the roofline and the neon words such as "footlong hot dogs" and "giant hamburgers" that are mesmerizing. The Paul Bunyan burger and other food is good, though fans come for the atmosphere, which includes speakerphone order boxes, carhops, and music in the lot.

The Parkette Drive In, opened in 1951, is known for its fried chicken and Kentucky Poor Boy double-decker cheeseburger. It is especially famous for its tall neon sign with a carhop and cars that appear to drive toward the restaurant. The Parkette closed in January 2003, and at the end of 2006, it was again for sale for $397,000 (not including the land), with the explanation that there were ten absentee owners, but one on-site

Left: The tremendous sign for the Parkette in Lexington, Kentucky, has been featured on its carry-out boxes.
Below: The Chick-Inn lights up the night in Ann Arbor, Michigan.

Bronco's in Omaha, Nebraska, features an exuberant 1950s roofline.

owner could revive the business, which includes inside seating and seventy-five carhop stations.

In Omaha, Nebraska, Bronco's Hamburgers calls out with its lasso-waving cowboy sign and curvy roof lined with fluorescent tubes. And just down Leavenworth Street is La Casa, with an Italian musician on its sign. Locals and groups such as 2020 Omaha have worked to inform the public about the value and beauty of such twentieth-century historic resources. At the Fat Boy Drive-In on Old Bath Road in Brunswick, Maine, near Bowdoin College, those wanting a big burger can ask their carhop for a Whoper—that's right, one "p," not two. It was originally a Whopper, but when Burger King challenged the drive-in, it solved the problem with the new spelling. Fans also rave about the lobster rolls and onion rings. It's been in the same family since the 1950s and is still a plain building with corrugated plastic awnings for shading cars, but locals know this is the real thing. At the K-N Root Beer drive-in restaurant in Amarillo, Texas, second-generation owner Sue Hill carries on with carhop service and a secret recipe to make root beer on-site several times a day, served in frosted mugs.

In Miami, Oklahoma, Waylan's Ku-Ku is the lone survivor of a chain of more than 200 drive-through restaurants. The buildings looked like cuckoo clocks, with a bird on top chiming each hour. The chain thrived throughout the Midwest.

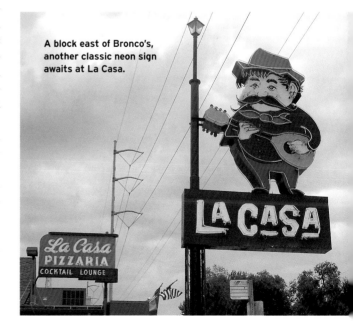

A block east of Bronco's, another classic neon sign awaits at La Casa.

The Ku-Ku in Miami, Oklahoma, is the last of a chain of that numbered more than 200. It's been in the Waylan family for three decades.

This location was bought more than thirty years ago by Eugene Waylan, who now owns the last of the ku-kus. Try the fried okra or fried green tomatoes. Wright's Dairy-Rite in Staunton, Virginia, has specialized in the double-patty Superburger since opening in 1952. Or try a Monster Burger, but customers are warned about this half-pounder: "This is our biggest burger, and requires the most cooking time. This is not the burger for those in a hurry."

The world's largest drive-in, and one of the best known, is The Varsity in Atlanta, Georgia. Located near the Georgia Tech campus since 1928, it covers more than two acres and can fit 600 cars or 800 people inside. On an average day, it may serve two *miles* of hot dogs, 300 gallons of

Wright's Dairy-Rite, founded in 1952 in Staunton, Virginia.

The fifty-six-foot-tall Big Chicken in Marietta, Georgia, is a landmark for both locals and pilots. MARTHA CARVER

chili, and 5,000 fried pies. But it's best known for the auctioneer-like calling of the staff: "What'll ya have? What'll ya have? What'll ya have? Have your order in your mind and your money in your hand!" Another location opened in downtown Athens in 1932 and was relocated in 1963, and there are now four others, including a Varsity Jr., which like the main one, still offers curb service.

Fans of franchise restaurants have numerous meccas to search out, from the few early McDonald's with old signs or even a pair of giant arches to Googie-style coffee shops. Some of the favorite places are related to Kentucky Fried Chicken. About fifteen miles north of Atlanta, the Big Chicken was built of sheet metal in 1963, when the place was Johnny Reb's. It stayed when KFC leased the place in 1974, but age and nesting birds led to its deterioration. A 1993 New Year's storm caused enough damage that the company decided

The orange roof was the roadside attraction for Howard Johnson's in the Boston area where I grew up in the 1950s. It was usually topped by a white cupola with a weather vane that featured a pieman and his dog, which also appeared, clearly outlined, in the great neon signs beside the restaurants. These spelled out "HOWARD JOHNSON'S" in diagonal Art Deco letters, and the zigzag S was a lightning bolt in pink.

We always called them by their full first and last name, in formal New England manners, never HoJos, as they were called much later. One was always just beyond the bend at a traffic rotary or major intersection. They were also being built along the new Route 128 superhighway around Boston and the Massachusetts Turnpike to New York, with a sleek, glass modern design to match the suburban ranch houses, but still capped by orange roofs.

It was the promise of fun food that drew us inside—the grilled hot dogs, fried clams, and twenty-eight flavors of ice cream, including my favorite, pistachio. We sang a little jingle just before we stopped: "On Route 128, where we sit and sat and ate, at Howard Johnson's!" The orange roof was always on my mind.

—ARTHUR KRIM, co-founder, Society for Commercial Archeology

A classic early style Howard Johnson's restaurant.

to tear it down rather than spend $200,000 on repairs, but when word got out, 8,000 fans called, and the company decided to rehab the giant sign with help from Pepsi-Cola. The store now sells souvenirs of the big bird in both wooden and "beanie" styles.

KFC got its start in Corbin, Kentucky, where Harland Sanders, an honorary Kentucky "colonel," opened a gas station and lunch room along U.S. 25, the Dixie Highway, in the early 1930s. He expanded to a much larger restaurant, where he perfected his secret recipe of eleven herbs and spices using a pressure cooker instead of the more common frying method. He also added a motel, and for those in doubt about staying at a roadside

court, he included a model room inside the restaurant to persuade customers to stay the night. When I-75 bypassed his place in 1956, business declined so much that he sold his holdings, and at age sixty-six, with only a Social Security check, Sanders hit the road. He'd begun a plan in 1952 to franchise others to sell his popular chicken, for which he'd get 5¢ a piece. By 1956, he had a dozen accounts; by decade's end, more than 200; and when he sold the business in 1964 for $2 million, more than 600. The restaurant here grew like any other KFC, and then to honor the hundredth birthday of the late Colonel in 1990, it was restored in the spirit of the early restaurant. Sanders Café and Museum has a modern food counter along with his re-created kitchen, the model motel room, and memorabilia such as carry-out buckets, Colonel-themed souvenirs, and a barrel of the secret recipe mixture.

There's also a museum in Salt Lake City at "the first KFC," founded in 1952 when Sanders dropped in on Leon "Pete" Harman, whom he'd met at a National Restaurant Association conference. In 1941, Pete and his wife, Arlene, had paid $700 for the Dew Drop, which had five booths and eight bar stools and specialized in two-for-15¢ hamburgers and 10¢ draft beers. It was here in 1952 at their Harman's Café that the Colonel cooked them a chicken dinner late one night. The Colonel proposed his franchising idea, Pete came up with the Kentucky Fried Chicken name, and by August, the Harman's Café rooftop sign was joined by a huge image of the Colonel and giant KFC buckets ringing the roofline. Pete got the Colonel to dress in white and make appearances to join his image to the brand. The original building expanded the next year, but it was demolished in 2004 and replaced with a much-larger Harman's Café filled with company memorabilia. Outside stand statues of the Colonel and Pete. It is now operated by Harman Management Company, which has more than 375 restaurants in the western United States and is KFC's largest domestic master franchise network. KFC itself has grown to more than 14,000 locations.

FAN FAVORITE

As a seven-year-old, I took it for granted that doughnuts would be sold out of a stucco shed topped with a two-story-high concrete doughnut. In Los Angeles where I grew up, the chance of driving by architecture that was slightly at odds with the bland linear landscape of the Southland's urban sprawl was more than a chance occurrence. I recall a giant bull dog crumbling away in Culver City and a giant hot dog near Hollywood. The Big Donut was just down the street in Inglewood, and although there were other neighborhood doughnut stands (we frequented one called Winchell's after Sunday Mass), special events were reserved for the Big Donut, where it still majestically stands. Anticipating the huge doughnut sign was part of the treat. That and the fact that you didn't have to get out of your car—it was a drive-up. I didn't realize it at the time but there were lots of Big Donuts scattered around L.A. Only three remain.

These days, I make fewer cholesterol-laden visits to the oversize pastry. Yet when returning to L.A. from traveling abroad, I instinctively peer out the jet window as I approach the airport, searching for the distinctive landmark. Once I spot Randy's Donuts, as it is now called, I know I am home.

—JIM HEIMANN, author of *California Crazy* and executive editor of *Taschen America*

Cherry pie is peeved! How come apple pie was chosen to symbolize our country in the expression "as American as apple pie?" Why is Thanksgiving represented by pumpkin, sweet potato, and even the less loved mincemeat? And what pie won the coveted spot of being the number-one choice to throw in someone's face? Banana cream, not cherry. Of all the pies to ever be grand-prize winner of the Pillsbury Bake-Off, there's apple, pecan, peach—even sesame, chocolate, and granola. But never a cherry.

Feeling like the ugly stepchild, relegated to the back of your grocer's freezer alongside blueberry and Boston cream, cherry's had enough. In America, where bigger is better, cherry pie decided to take matters into its own hands.

Have you ever seen the world's largest sweet potato pie? World's largest lemon meringue pie? You have not.

Cherry pie *finally* rules! And by the looks of the almost empty pie tin I came upon in Charlevoix, Michigan, its plan worked. No one can stay away from the tastiest pie in all the land.

I've got dibs on the last piece!

—HILLARY CARLIP, author of *Queen of the Oddballs: And Other True Stories from a Life Unaccording to Plan*, www.hillarycarlip.com

Hillary at the big cherry pie slice and its awning—what every pie pan needs for proper protection. Other towns have since taken the "largest cherry pie crown," but Charlevoix, Michigan, keeps its sign. It *was* first, after all, and it still has a piece of pie, albeit concrete.

The newest KFC roadside attraction is in Rachel, Nevada. To launch a new look for its logo and stores late in 2006, KFC built an 87,500-square foot image of the Colonel, replacing his classic white, double-breasted suit with a red apron. It took nearly a month to manufacture the 65,000 one-foot-square pieces, then six days to assemble them under cover. It was originally to be in the Utah desert near the site of the first KFC, Harman's, but when a torrential downpour rendered the site inaccessible, it was moved to the Area 51 desert along NV 375—the Extraterrestrial Highway—to play up the fact that the logo can be seen from outer space. A satellite photo at www.kfc.com shows the logo from 423 miles above the earth, easily visible to passing spaceships.

SPOTLIGHT ON
Diners

Diners seem to bring out the best in people. Although many a café and hometown restaurant has similar qualities, we're speaking of restaurants manufactured and moved to their places of business. A diner usually has a counter with swiveling stools, and classic models have the griddle behind the counter, which encourages lots of conversation. The best-loved models are from the mid-twentieth century, when the proper proportions of chrome, neon, and stainless steel reached their apogee. Therein lies the reason for their popularity: Different diner styles and brands look enough alike to offer familiarity, yet with few being part of a chain, each simmers with its own strong local identity and specialties. They offer a comforting environment, whether you're a regular or far from home.

The diner industry began in New England to serve late-night factory workers. As industrialization spread south, so did the diner industry, settling around New York City and northern New Jersey. Transporting diners more than a couple hundred miles was prohibitively expensive, so not many are found beyond the Appalachian Mountains. Few from before 1920 have survived, but a small number from that decade still operate. Franks Diner in Kenosha, Wisconsin, claims to be the country's oldest continuously operating lunch car. Old-timers recall its being pulled here in 1926 by six horses.

Fans like to explain that diners are not old railroad or trolley cars, but in fact, as electric trolleys replaced horse-drawn ones, many an entrepreneur bought a discarded one for a pittance, added a kitchen and seats, and went into the diner business. Many closed just as quickly. Angel's Diner in Palatka, Florida, is the state's oldest railroad dining car turned restaurant, opened in 1932 with ten stools and six tables. It's always busy, with folks lining up for BLTs, fried okra, and Dreamsicle shakes. The place is a mix of stained glass, neon, red vinyl seats, black-and-white tile floors, and Coke memorabilia inside. Curb service is offered too.

Some operators who didn't have the money for or interest in factory-built diners made theirs themselves. The best known, more so than many a factory model, is Moody's Diner on U.S. 1 in Waldoboro, Maine. The diner, a long white restaurant with clapboard siding, has been greatly enlarged, until today it seats 104. Its origins go back to Percy Moody, who built three tourist cabins here in 1927. He added a lunchroom in 1930, but when the road was bypassed in 1934, he moved his access road to the new route and placed a food stand there, the start of the current restaurant. During their seventy-fifth celebration in 2002, thirty-one family members were involved, many of them great-grandchildren. The cabins and motel fill in the summer, as does the diner. Their formula is pretty simple: good food, reasonable prices, and quick, pleasant service.

If one diner is not enough, you'll find four in one spot about fifteen miles north of Grand Rapids, Michigan.

Rockford, Michigan, sports three diners plus a good-looking replica (at right) and lots of homemade food.

The Palace is Maine's oldest diner. It opened for business in 1927, the year Charles Lindbergh hopped the Atlantic in his *Spirit of St. Louis* and the Babe walloped his monumental sixty home runs—when that still meant something.

If you arrive at the Palace early enough, you may hear French being spoken. In days of old, it was almost all French. Customers, so the story goes, would greet proprietor Orville Pollard with a hearty "How are you?" in French. But try as he might, Orville just could not pronounce the expected "Très bien." He could, however, say, "Three beers." Patrons loved it.

The Palace supposedly got its name when one of the builders said, "Wow! This looks like a little palace." It still does, and a rare little palace at that. It is the only known surviving diner constructed by a small Lowell, Massachusetts, diner manufacturer named Pollard and Company.

The Palace is still a joyous sight to behold, and it serves darned good food! It's a must visit if you're motoring along Maine's beautiful coast.

—WILL ANDERSON, author of books on Maine, New England, and pop culture topics such as baseball, basketball, breweriana, and roadside architecture.

The Palace is Maine's oldest diner and the only known survivor made by Pollard. WILL ANDERSON

Artist Jerry Berta started the collection, known sometimes as Diner Land or Diner World, in 1987, when he brought Uncle Bob's Diner (1947 O'Mahoney) from Flint and reopened it as a studio and gallery called The Diner Store. With drivers constantly stopping for a meal, he brought in another in 1991. Rosie's is named for its role in 1970s Bounty paper towel commercials. (Only those over thirty will instantly recall Nancy Davis as waitress Rosie demonstrating the "quicker picker upper.") The diner began as The Silver Dollar Diner (1946 Paramount) in Little Ferry, New Jersey, where the commercials were filmed, hence its renaming in the 1970s.

Berta did it again in 1994, when he brought the Garden of Eatin' (1952 Silk City) from Fulton, New York. The fourth diner was actually home-built as an addition.

Berta attempted a chain of Rosie's before he began scaling back. After various stints at running this site, he finally sold it in 2006 to Randy and Jonelle Roest. Berta remains a regular and rents his studio diner from them. Regulars are pleased that the food is again top-rate, offering everything from foot-long hot dogs and fried bologna sandwiches (a favorite of Jonelle's dad) to dinners like roast turkey or beef and egg noodles, a recipe from her Jonelle's grandmother. The Roests also con-

Perhaps the most distinctive Valentine-brand diner anywhere, the King's Chef in Colorado Springs has a castle theme. This thirteen-seater, opened in 1956, has been run since 1997 by Gary Geiser, who takes great pride in his place and even bottles his own green chili. Watch out—it's spicy!

verted the adjacent diner into The Bar at Rosie's Diner, with seven high-definition flat-panel televisions and a mahogany pool table. This home-built diner has no food service, and out back, a mini-golf with giant food for obstacles languishes, though we expect customers will again be golfing around the big burger and slab of pie.

A few manufacturers popped up around Lake Erie to serve the cities west of the mountains, and interestingly, the most easily identifiable diner brand was built in Kansas. Valentine Diners were small, to fit the smaller towns that were their market. Easily identifiable by their small size, angular styling, and handful of stools, they're found mostly in the Midwest and Southwest, many of them along Route 66.

As for bringing out the best in people, a good example is O'Rourke's Diner in Middletown, Connecticut. This small eatery has been in the same family since its purchase from the Mountain View factory in 1946 and is listed in the National Register of Historic Places. Owner Brian O'Rourke is known far and wide for his hospitality, generosity, and culinary variety. When a fire in August 2006 gutted the place, it turned out Brian had no fire insurance. Within three months, fans from across the globe had collected $100,000, and this was before a *New York Times* feature. Contractors are donating services, and many people are helping with fund-raisers in hopes that sometime soon, Brian will once again serve his famed steamed cheeseburgers.

CHAPTER 6

ADVENTURES WITH ART

Eccentrics follow their muse, and tourists follow the eccentrics. Art can be found almost anywhere, from lovingly decorated mailboxes to houses made from cans or bottles. Most are the creations of lone visionaries, either to make a statement or just express themselves. One of the best known is the Garden of Eden in Lucas, Kansas, just off beautiful U.S. 24, where S. P. Dinsmore created a 3-D vision of biblical characters and his populist views. The cement sculptures run from the Devil to Adam and Eve to "Labor Crucified," where a doctor, preacher, lawyer, and banker surround the personification of working people. The site sells a wonderful reproduction of Dinsmoor's own *Pictorial History of the Cabin Home in Garden of Eden*. At the time of writing in 1927, he had used more than 113 tons of cement for the above characters plus trees, a dining hall, animal cages, three U.S. flags, and other creations, even an overhead sign. Visitors can even see Dinsmoor in his all-cement, three-story, log-cabin-shaped mausoleum, resting in a cement coffin under a glass lid. Though it is mostly men who have brought their artistic

Biblical and allegorical figures are found throughout S. P. Dinsmoor's Garden of Eden in Lucas, Kansas, such as this snake giving an apple to Eve.

World's Largest Ball of Twine in Cawker City, Kansas. The yellow line is the start of the Masterpiece Twine Walk.

obsessions to the roadside, visitors are welcomed to Lucas by the World's Largest Souvenir Plate, designed and painted by Erika Nelson.

Along the same line is Wisconsin Concrete Park, an outdoor museum of conrete sculptures embellished with colored pieces of glass. Farmer, musician, and lumberjack Fred Smith began his self-taugh craft at age sixty-five and built 237 figures of animals and historic scenes between 1950 and 1964. You'll find Abraham Lincoln, the Statue of Liberty, Kit Carson, a farmer with oxen, and even the Anheuser-Busch Clydesdale team. Smith's "gift to the American people" is now maintained by the nonprofit Friends of Fred Smith.

With the Midwest as a nexus for roadside attractions, it's fitting that the battle for Largest

FAN FAVORITE

The art and architecture of the Italian Renaissance aren't lost on the roadside fans of Illinois. In the Chicago suburb of Niles, a half-scale replica of the Leaning Tower of Pisa is quite an attention getter, but unlike its predecessor constructed 600 years earlier, this tower leans on purpose. It was constructed in 1933-34 as a water tower to supply swimming pools built by industrialist Robert Ilg for his employees. It rises more than 90 feet tall and leans just over 7 feet off plumb. Noted San Francisco architect Albert Farr was heavily criticized for creating the structure, which became known as Farr's Folly.

Today the replica tower leans outside the Niles YMCA building. A reflecting pool, an old-fashioned phone booth, and beautiful landscaping all enhance the site. It's perfect for a fun photo op, and the authentic Italian music wafting through the air from a hidden sound system creates an ambience visitors won't soon forget.

—MIKE "BIG TOMATO" GASSMANN, president and CEO of the World's Largest Catsup Bottle Fan Club, www.catsupbottle.com

Mike Gassmann tries a quick, if imaginary, fix to straighten the Leaning Tower of Niles, Illinois.
JUDY DEMOISY

The Orange Show was an ongoing creation by Jeff McKissack from 1956 until his death in 1980 to honor his favorite fruit and illustrate his belief that longevity results from hard work and good nutrition. Like many folk artists, he used common building materials and found objects, building a maze of walkways, arenas, and exhibits decorated with mosaics and painted iron figures. It is now the site of many art and music programs. DEBRA JANE SELTZER

Ball of Twine is between Minnesota and Kansas. The Darwin, Minnesota, ball was started in 1950 by Francis A. Johnson, who wrapped for four hours every day for twenty-nine years. Now preserved in its own gazebo across from the town park, it's the largest ball spun by one person. It also served as the inspiration for Frank Stoeber, who started his own twine ball three years later. Stoeber's ball is now at the center of his hometown, Cawker City, Kansas, and folks can add their own pieces, making it truly the biggest ball of twine—though Minnesotans will point out that this ball was spun by more than one. Indeed, if out-of-staters are driving through this part of northern Kansas, it's the big ball that's bringing them to the town of about 520, though touring scenic U.S. 24 is reason enough. The ball's sign, not updated since 1988, gives the circumference as more than forty feet. A recent effort to keep folks here for more than a few snapshots is the Masterpiece Twine Walk, a painted path of twine that takes you past storefronts with art master-pieces reinterpreted to include twine, such as the *Mona Lisa* holding a twine ball. Across the street, Lottie Herod runs an antique store filled with twine ball gifts, most made herself from fired clay. Why all this fuss about twine? Though mostly replaced by wire now, it once was widely used to wrap hay bales, and farmers would roll up scraps of twine so animals wouldn't eat them and to keep them from tangling in machinery.

Such passion is the motivation behind many roadside attractions. The Watts Towers in the Watts district of Los Angeles are amazingly tall and complex, yet they were all built by one man using no machinery, scaffolding, bolts, rivets, or welds. The seventeen towers—two of them ninety-nine feet tall—were handcrafted from 1921 to 1955 by Sabato "Simon" Rodia, an evangelical minister in a Mexican tent-revival church, as a tribute to the spirit of those who make their dreams tangible. He called them Nuestro Pueblo, or "our town." He used steel pipes, rebar, and wire mesh coated in concrete that he embedded with seashells, broken glass, pottery, tile—anything others considered disposable—and decorated with bigger items such as bike parts and bed frames. Tired of abuse from neighbors, Rodia left here in 1955. The towers' fame and support grew, but the city nonetheless ordered them destroyed, so the owners allowed the city to conduct a stability test. A steel cable was tied to each tower, and a crane tried to pull them over, but the towers endured, not even wavering, until the crane itself failed. The site is now operated by the city's Cultural Affairs Department as Simon Rodia State Historical Park. The Watts Towers Arts Center gives tours of the site for a small fee.

Just as prolific was Howard Finster, who turned a two-and-a-half-acre swamp next to his house into one of the most famous sculpture gardens. Starting in 1960, he spent seven years filling what had been the town dump for Pennville,

Fields of the Wood in Murphy, North Carolina, has monuments dedicated to the Bible, notably the Ten Commandments sprawled across a hillside. CLAUDETTE STAGER

Georgia. He grew flowers and vegetables, calling it the Plant Farm Museum, but others began calling it Paradise Gardens. It became the artist's vision of Eden, built of trash but espousing biblical passages in hopes of connecting people with God. Like Rodia, he embedded his sculptures with discarded materials such as broken dishes, pieces of glass, even bike chains. He used Coke bottles to build the walls of a small house. His family ran it after his death, but now it's run by a Christian-affiliated nonprofit organization.

Religious inspiration among roadside artists is common. The Ave Maria Grotto in Cullman, Alabama, is known as "Jerusalem in Miniature." The four-acre park features 125 small-scale reproductions of well-known historic buildings and shrines, such as ones from Jerusalem and the Holy Land, Roman landmarks like the Colosseum, and Spanish missions of the American Southwest along a walking trail. They were built by Brother Joseph Zoettl, a Benedictine monk of St. Bernard Abbey. At the center is an artificial cave, the Ave Maria Grotto. On an even grander scale is Fields of the Wood Bible Park, west of Chattanooga, Tennessee, where you'll find the world's largest Ten Commandments. A century ago, Ambrose Jessup Tomlinson hiked a mountain here to pray and came back saying that God had told him to form what became the Church of God of Prophecy, now with more than 700,000

This half-size Stonehenge on the campus of the University of Missouri in Rolla was dedicated by a Druid priest on the summer solstice of 1984.

members in 115 countries. He wished to mark the spot of the revelation, so his new church bought 210 acres, including an adjacent mountain where he began the commandments. After his death, the letters were upgraded to concrete, each 5 feet tall and 4 feet wide. Other landmarks include the world's largest altar (80 feet long), the world's largest New Testament (an open concrete Bible 30 by 50 feet), and the world's largest cross (115 by 150 feet), plus other biblical replicas such as Christ's tomb.

Perhaps less inspired by religion than the desire to imitate a famous wonder, replicas of Stonehenge had no trouble making the leap across the Atlantic. Whereas England has but one, high atop the Salisbury Plain, America has several wanna-bes. A full-scale Stonehenge in southern Washington State overlooking the Columbia River was the first monument in the United States to honor World War I soldiers, and it now also honors those of the wars that have followed. Local entrepreneur Samuel Hill had purchased 6,000 acres in 1907 to establish a Quaker agricultural community. Hill, a pacifist, mistakenly believed that the original Stonehenge had been used as a sacrificial site, so he built a replica as a reminder that "humanity is still being sacrificed to the god of war."

A half-scale Stonehenge at the University of Missouri in Rolla was meant to honor the abilities of the region's stonecutters as well as the school's mining and engineering disciplines. The only granite quarry in Missouri was closed when rock was needed in 1983, so the 160 tons of gran-

Visitors are mesmerized by a seventeen-foot-long animated woodcarving of old-world Eastern Europe at Slovak Folk Crafts in Grove City, Pennsylvania.

ite was obtained from Elberton, Georgia. This was the first major structure to be carved using high-pressure water jets.

Elberton has what's called "America's Stonehenge," which recalls the original but is quite different. The Georgia Guidestones are nineteen-foot-tall slabs that have messages inscribed promoting harmony between people. The massive monument is made from six granite slabs: a central one, four around it, and one with explanatory text. Ten principles are inscribed in eight modern languages. Ordered and paid for anonymously, the monument was unveiled in 1980. The granite stones, including the capstone announcing "Let These Be Guides to an Age of Reason" in four ancient languages, seem to be nondenominational, and indeed they get visitors from across the spectrum of beliefs.

Not every artistic creation draws its inspiration from biblical or mystical sources. Slovak Folk Crafts north of Pittsburgh has the largest collection of Slovak-made handicrafts in the United States, but it's the animated woodcarving that puts it in the class of roadside attractions. Owners Dave and Anne Dayton aren't Slovak themselves, but they fell in love with Slovakia and

its people. They import pottery, hand-cut crystal, wooden toys, and intricately cut and decorated eggs. This led to their most impressive piece, a seventeen-foot-wide scene depicting folk life in Slovakia as it's existed for hundreds of centuries. It took three carvers more than two years to make the buildings and eighty-two moving figures.

Some artistic projects are a community effort, and many vintage attractions were job relief programs during the Depression. That's the case in Lemmon, South Dakota, where Petrified Wood Park not only gave the town a beautiful attraction, but also employed a few dozen men from 1930 to 1932. An amateur geologist helped them gather fossils locally. Most pieces are built from petrified wood, though they also include round rocks from North Dakota's Cannonball River. The result is a museum, a wishing well, and hundreds of pile sculptures, including 100 conical ones, some twenty feet tall. They somewhat resemble trees and are decorated yearly for a Fantasyland display. A castle-shaped building was made with thousands of pounds of petrified dinosaur and mammoth bones.

The most heart-wrenching of the artistic roadside attractions is surely Coral Castle in Home-

Petrified Wood Park was created in the 1930s along an entire block in Lemmon, South Dakota, and restored in 2002.
MARK HUFSTETLER

stead, Florida, an homage by Edward Leedskalnin to his sweetheart, Agnes Scuffs, who broke up with him on the eve of their wedding. Though small in stature, Ed built the house, furniture, walls, and decorative gardens from more than 1,100 tons of coral from 1923 until his death in 1951, using no large machinery or outside help. Though he did come from a family of stone masons, it's remarkable that he was able to move, let alone carve, such huge, heavy pieces. Ed said only that he knew the secrets used to build the ancient pyramids. He died a single man, and Agnes never did visit. The gift shop offers audio and video tours, plus souvenirs such as coasters, dish towels, keychains, shot glasses, spoons, sun visors, tote bags, tropical-themed colognes, candles, hand creams, and jewelry. Visitors can also get the complete collection of Ed's writings, which includes *Sweet Sixteen*, *Cosmic Force*, and *Mineral, Vegetable and Animal Life*.

A much lighter approach was taken by Amarillo helium tycoon Stanley Marsh 3, who likes pranks. He invited a collective of artists called Ant Farm to create a work in his wheat field six miles west of town. In *Automerica* (1976), artist Chip Lord wrote of what became the Cadillac Ranch:

In May 1974 we went to Amarillo and began buying Cadillacs. It was a white-trash dream come true, buying and driving old Cadillacs on the windswept plains of the Texas Panhandle. In our search we visited every used-car lot in Amarillo and most of the junkyards. . . . We found a silver '49 fastback but the guy was asking $700

Shannon Rodriguez drove from California to the Cadillac Ranch, west of Amarillo, Texas, to create and photograph a message for her dad: "He always says 'It's always something' about nearly everything." Here she preps the 1949 coupe.

Shannon's finished work. This photo can be seen at http://xvshanissa.deviantart.com/prints, along with a nice view of the entire Cadillac Ranch lineup.

for it, a price we considered exorbitant (the cars averaged $200 apiece). Stanley suggested we buy it and then smash up the front end with sledgehammers in front of the proud previous owner. So we did in fact smash it, with the cameras rolling as the bewildered owner winced in agony. . . . The hired backhoe operator was a bit perplexed by the task at hand but he dug, where we told him, a hole eight feet deep. Then we showed him to use the bucket of his tractor to lift up the car until it slid into the hole.

The cars range from that 1949 Club Coupe to a 1963 Sedan. (By the way, the owner of the 1949 "Sedanette" was invited to the opening ceremony on June 21, 1974, to see that there was method to the madness.) The original paint jobs were long ago covered by graffiti and now regularly get repainted. In 1997, the cars were moved two miles west further to escape sprawl (yes, even on the Texas prairie). In the ultimate compliment, the site was reportedly re-created twice in the 1990s: once near Mojave, California, for a Chrysler of Canada TV commercial, and again outside of Austin, Texas, for the 1996 film *Cadillac Ranch*. In *Cars*, Pixar artists paid homage with the distant Cadillac Range mountains mimicking the ranch's finned rear ends.

Marsh also commissioned the lesser-known Amarillo Ramp fifteen miles northwest of town.

Artist Robert Smithson was killed in a plane crash while surveying the site. Sonic Youth guitarist Lee Ranaldo honored him with a 1998 CD, *Amarillo Ramp (for Robert Smithson)*. And south of town are the Legs of Ozymandias, which includes a fake roadside historical marker about Mary Shelley coming upon the giant pair in 1819 and being moved to write about them. The legs were recently repainted with sports socks.

SPOTLIGHT ON
Souvenirs

Many souvenir shops claim to be the largest in their state. The Fort Cody Trading Post in North Platte, Nebraska, is one in a long line of gift shops owned by the Henline family. The ones they've had in this city all played up the Buffalo Bill theme, as Bill Cody built his Scouts Rest home and barn on the north edge of town. Fort Cody offers sweatshirts, books, moccasins, cowboy hats, and other western wear, plus cap guns, rubber snakes, and all those other things you always wanted your parents to buy. Some 20,000 handcarved figures and props, many animated, re-create Buffalo Bill's famed Wild West Show in miniature. Out back, kids can run around Wild West props.

In Colorado, the claimant to largest gift shop is Garden of the Gods Trading Post, similarly filled with all sorts of souvenirs. The 1,391-acre Garden of the Gods Park, named for its stunning red sandstone formations, is operated by the city of Colorado Springs and has a new visitors center. The trading post was founded in the 1920s as a Pueblo curio museum, employing regional Native Americans to craft baskets and pottery or per-

The Canyon Trading Post, established in 1889 on the road north from Willams, Arizona, to the Grand Canyon, includes a gift shop, gas station, restaurant, and convenience store.

form dances. Such local flavor is played up by most souvenir shops and is especially evident in trading posts of the Southwest, where giant kachinas stand at the roadside to lure in travelers. In the South, shops are often filled with souvenirs that embrace southern cultural clichés: Confederate flags, Mammy salt and pepper shakers, hillbilly humor, and country music. The handful of Ozarkland stores are not any more over the top than

Lottie Herod with a friend at her Great Plains Art Gallery in Cawker City, Kansas, the place to go for Ball of Twine teapots, snow domes, magnets, postcards, salt and pepper shakers, hats, shirts, and a stylish rock-and-twine ball combo. When we stopped, Lottie was at home baking up more crafts in her kiln.

FAN FAVORITE

Prairie Dog Town in Oakley, Kansas, is one of the last of the dying breed of old-school snake farms. After you plunk down your admission fee, you are treated to a glorious menagerie of animal displays, including a pen of rattlesnakes, dozens of stuffed two-headed critters, and a petting zoo. Outside, you need to dodge the critter landmines and avoid the burrows made by hundreds of resident prairie dogs. The gift shop is the pièce de résistance, with T-shirts, tomahawks, and other souvenirs. I can't wait to go back!

—FRANK BRUSCA, webmaster of Route40.net

Tooling along the long and lonely U.S. Highway 93 in northwestern Arizona, keep your eyes open and your camera ready. You don't want to miss classic roadside attractions such as Rose's Den, a truckers' café dating from the construction of the nearby Hoover Dam in the 1930s, or Santa Claus, with its Christmas-themed architecture and goods, now closed and for sale. My favorite stop along this desert highway is Grasshopper Junction, a "town" primarily consisting of a tacky oasis gift shop and gas station decorated with funky insect-themed murals that always attract photo-happy tourists. If lucky, they also get to witness a western shootout with the Dolan Gang.

—DOUGLAS TOWNE, roadside photographer, writer, and editor, www.sem20.com/neonmotel

Doug's wife, Maureen Towne, poses next to a gun-slinging, pick-ax-wielding, prospecting blue grasshopper at an Arizona roadside oasis south of Hoover Dam.
DOUGLAS TOWNE

similar gift shops but nonetheless manage to generate either passion for them or mocking of the kitsch that awaits inside.

Food is perhaps the most common kind of souvenir. Pecans have long been a staple of southern food stands, corn reigns in the Midwest, and pistachios can be bought in New Mexico. Florida's welcome centers have always been ready to help tourists take home a crate of oranges. At Orange World near Orlando, the store itself is an attraction, the fiberglass dome roof looking like a massive half orange. Family-owned since 1973 and orange-shaped since the 1980s, it specializes in Indian River fruit but is still primarily a gift shop full of candies, jellies, T-shirts, and most anything with a Florida or Disney theme.

Perry's Tropical Nut House in Belfast, Maine, opened in 1927 when Irving Perry began selling pecans he had bought in the South, hence the "tropical" name. New owners in 1939 expanded the business to include mountains of nuts from around the world, a nut museum, and giant animal statues in the parking lot as well as inside, most famously a "man-killer clam." The store also became famous as a gift shop, selling souvenirs to fit the tropical theme. It was closed and auctioned in 1997 with the idea that condos would be built on the site, but the Nut House survived and recently came under the ownership of George and Ellen Darling and their daughter Kim O'Brien, who are reviving the business. The focus has shifted from the tropics to regional products, though some of those parking-lot animals still beckon travelers.

Route 66 remains home to a number of trading posts. The biggest gathering is along the Arizona–New Mexico border astride old Route 66 and I-40. Most famous, but looking closed recently, is the Chief Yellowhorse, opened by former Navy airman and policeman Juan Yellowhorse when he bought the Miller Trading Post in

Ozarkland stores are renowned for their offbeat gifts, many with a hillbilly theme.

Gazell Stewart and a young relative work the counter at Stewart's Petrified Wood Shop in Holbrook, Arizona.

1960. The Chief Yellowhorse was known for years by its many billboards, and nearby competitors also trade on its name—one even has a little yellow horse on the roof—but Juan died in 1999, and recently the post looks deserted. Farther west near Holbrook, you can scrounge through piles of geodes or feed the ostriches at Stewart's Petrified Wood Shop. The dinosaurs and scantily clad female mannequins draw a steady stream of the curious from those driving I-40 to the nearby Painted Desert.

Perhaps souvenirs aren't your bag, and you prefer shopping for antiques, but not just your run-of-the-mill dust catchers. A pair of shops in Washington State offer offbeat gifts intermixed with all the oddball curiosities you'll ever want to see. Travelers passing Marsh's Free Museum in Long Beach can tell by the re-created half man, half alligator on the roof that they're in for a treat. You'll find endless oddities here—most famously, Jake the Alligator Man, who even has his

Eli Sfassie got the idea to top his Orange World gift shop near Orlando, Florida, with a massive orange while sitting in the Waffle Shop next door. RICK SEBAK

In the late 1960s, my parents would pack up all three girls in the station wagon and head west. A fond memory was the visits to a great Indian trading post in Ogallala, Nebraska, on U.S. 30, the Lincoln Highway.

Mom would always encourage Dad to stop here. Boy was I glad because the Ogallala Trading Post was cool, with Indian jewelry, feather headdresses, and tomahawks.

I remember well my tomahawk. It was a doozy. It wasn't rubber but had a real wooden handle, like a thick branch from a tree, and a real stone at the top for chopping something or somebody. There was also a thin layer of dripping fake blood on the stone and handle. My mother reminded me not to hurt anyone.

On subsequent visits, I chose a drum and a small Indian headdress with pretty colored feathers.

Sometime in the 1970s, we drove new I-80, making a special stop in Ogallala, but the trading post was closed. I was extremely disappointed.

—SHELLEE GRAHAM, photographer and author of *Tales from The Coral Court: Photos and Stories from a Lost Route 66 Landmark* and *Return to Route 66*, www.coralcourt.com

Shellee Graham, at five years old, visiting the Ogallala Trading Post. "Can you tell I am very proud of my new Indian souvenirs? I *loved* Indians and was very enthusiastic to stop at the trading posts. In some ways, I am still the same way today. I have been studying Native American jewelry, the hallmarks, the artists."
SHELLEE GRAHAM

Jackie Rosmus checks out Jake the Alligator Man at Marsh's Free Museum in Long Beach, Washington.
JONATHAN CHARD

own fan club. Other items include animal mounts, a human skeleton, a two-headed calf, Philippine corals, an eight-legged lamb, and antique amusements such as the Mills Violano-Virtuoso music box, which automatically plays a real violin and piano.

Fans of Jake might also want to check out a similar-looking mermaid not too far away at Ye Olde Curio Shop on Puget Sound in Seattle. It's in the same vein, with novelty gifts and repulsive but intriguing attractions including shrunken heads and mummified bodies, such as Sylvester and Sylvia. You'll also find totem poles, Eskimo carvings, wooden postcards, Viking helmets, hunting trophies, the Lord's Prayer on a grain of rice, and endless stacks of curios and novelties. Founded in 1899 by J. E. Standley, and named for the 1841 Charles Dickens novel, it's still in the same family and has been at Pier 54 since 1988. Both this and Marsh's have always been free. They know you'll stop for the novelty and most likely go home with a souvenir.

CHAPTER 7

INTRIGUING ACCOMMODATIONS

On December 12, 1925, Pasadena architect Arthur Heineman opened a new form of lodging on U.S. 101 in San Luis Obispo, California. He described it as "hoteldom in bungalows" and called it the Motel Inn, creating "motel" by merging "motor hotel." It's the kind of crazy wordplay that lots of entrepreneurs try, but this one stuck. Who would have thought it would come to represent a huge market niche of convenient roadside lodging that distinguishes itself from formal hotels typically found in cities where cars are separated from their owners? Being that travelers in 1925 might not yet get the distinction,

Heineman had a neon sign alternate between "Hotel" and "Motel."

The idea evolved over time and merged with the concept of tourist cabins; after World War II, cabins often were linked together under a common roof. By 1960, many a motel had turned away from rustic roots to embrace the supersonic future. The Satellite Motel in Omaha, Nebraska, took it a step further, getting styling cues from the space program. Likewise for the Stovall's Space Age Lodge near Disneyland in California and in Gila Bend, Arizona, both built by developer Al Stovall. Each building (part of the Best Western

The Satellite Motel has landed in Omaha!

chain) embraced Jetsons-style futuristic architecture and was loaded with rockets and outer space imagery. Katella Avenue in Anaheim was especially filled with space-age architecture, playing directly off such Disneyland attractions as the House of the Future. After that attraction closed in 1967, many themed establishments remodeled, and that city now actively promotes a more modern look—that is, current modern, not half-century-old modern. While the Arizona motel retains some space-age touches, the California location now sports tropical decor.

Many a traveler liked the idea of a motel but carried it with them in the form of a trailer, ready whenever they wanted to stop for the night. Taking the idea to its extreme, the Shady Dell, in the remote Mule Mountains of the southeastern corner of Arizona, features vintage trailers restored and set permanently as its rooms. There are nine midcentury travel trailers plus a 1947 Chris Craft Yacht and a 1947 bus remade in tiki style, and two more vintage trailers are rented monthly. It was started as a lark when two antique dealers began buying old trailers. After they placed them on an old tourist camp lot, they decided to try opening them to the public. A 1996 *New York Times* article, "Trailer Court in a Time Warp," by roadside journalists Jane and Michael Stern, brought streams of customers and curious people. Dot's Diner was added after being found abandoned outside Los Angeles. The ten-stool Valentine-brand diner had opened on the corner of Ventura and Topanga Canyon Boulevards in 1957 as Burger Bar #3. The town of Bisbee once thrived on copper mining, but it declined and today is revitalizing as an artists' enclave. The Shady Dell fits right in. New owners took over in 2004 but had to split their time between here and Alaska. It is once again for sale, listed in 2006 at $795,000 for the acre-and-a-half complex.

For many motels now and in years past, such a gimmick is used to draw customers. For some, it's as simple as the name. In Albuquerque near the Old Town district, the Monterey Non-Smokers Motel offers just what its name says, a smoke-free environment. Rooms at the Crowne Plaza Quaker Square in Akron, Ohio, are round, being inside the old grain silos. The thirty-six silos, 120 feet tall and 24 feet in diameter, were built in 1932, but when Quaker moved to Chicago in 1970, production ceased. Five years later, the redeveloped site opened.

A thirty-five-foot-tall beagle in Cottonwood, Idaho, draws customers and shutterbugs to the Dog Bark Park Inn, overlooking U.S. 95 between Lewiston and Grangeville. The couple that owns

Dot's Diner and vintage trailers offer a step back in time at the Shady Dell RV park. JEFF JENSEN, bygonebyways.com

The Dog Bark Park Inn, a bed-and-breakfast in Cottonwood, Idaho. MARTHA CARVER

it, Dennis and Frances, run a woodworking business specializing in dog-shaped souvenirs: Dennis carves them and Frances paints them. They opened Dog Bark Park first, and the inn is their ultimate creation.

In Willow Creek, California, Wyatt's gets lots more attention now that it's been renamed the

Bigfoot Motel. The town is far from population centers, but that makes sense—if there is a Bigfoot, he or she would spurn civilization. And it's here in northwest California that the Bigfoot legend thrives best. A local newspaper coined the term in 1958, when footprints were found at a construction site. When the crew foreman died, his family revealed it was all a prank, but the leg-

This cage at the Bigfoot Motel in Willow Creek, California, once housed a Bigfoot replica . . . but it's disappeared, just the like the real, or imagined, thing. ROBERT DESALVO

Like the Movie Manor Motel in Colorado, the Greenland Theatre Motel on U.S. 1 in Machias, Maine, featured "free movies in every room."

end had already caught fire, fed by a 1967 film from just north of town showing a big creature. The leading researcher's materials were donated to the Willow Creek–China Flat Museum, which added a wing in 1998 to house the collection. The town gladly embraces Bigfoot, whether real or imagined, with statues and lots of businesses

The Royal Hawaiian in Baker, California, gets mixed reviews but high points for style. JENNIFER BARON

adopting the name. Highway 96 starting in Willow Creek and heading north is even designated the Bigfoot Highway, or Bigfoot Scenic Highway.

Can't decide where to stay after your drive-in movie? No problem at Kelloff's Best Western Movie Manor in southern Colorado. Most of the rooms face the screen and are of course able to pick up the sound. It opened in 1955 as the Star Drive-In Theater, but with drive-ins declining a decade later, the motel was added. There are even two runways for a fly-in, drive-in experience. For those on the East Coast, you can try a motel movie at the Fairlee Drive-In and Motel in Vermont. All twelve rooms have a window (and shower window, if you're tall enough) facing the screen. The large theater opened in 1950 and reportedly added the motel in 1960; an old washing machine in the projection booth remains from when the original owner washed motel linens while the films ran. Both show movies from early May to at least the end of September.

Some try a theme to lure customers. Baker is the midpoint for those needing gas or cigarettes on the way from Los Angeles to Vegas or those needing to sober up on the way home. Most people stop because it's the *only* place to stop in the middle of the Mojave Desert. Fans of roadside giants will find an oversize thermometer announcing the region's high temperatures. It's 134 feet tall, one foot for every degree on the town's hottest day ever recorded in the United States, in nearby Death Valley on July 10, 1913. Arne's Royal Hawaiian Hotel advertises its "Thermometer View." The hotel was a key setting in the 2003 film *The Big Empty*, about strange doings in the desert. The other place roadside fans stop in town is the Bun Boy Restaurant, founded in 1926 and remodeled now but retaining a 1950s sign. Since becoming a partner in the 1950s, Will Herron had dreamed of a huge thermometer, finally realizing his dream in 1991. The complex in its shadow includes a motel (online reviews lean toward "grim"), twenty-four-hour restaurant, and store famous as the leading location for state Super Lotto millionaire winners.

By far the most famous, and earliest, motel to use themed rooms is the Madonna Inn, in San Luis Obispo, California, where the 108 rooms are each decorated in a different style. Not all are outrageous, though you'll often find carpet, walls, linens, furniture, even the restaurant's french toast, in startling shades of pink, and rocks from the adjacent hill were built into walls, floors, even showers. The motel was started with twelve rooms in 1958 by Alex and Phyllis Madonna.

The best-known accommodation in San Luis Obispo, California, is the Caveman Room at the Madonna Inn. PHYLLIS MADONNA

What do you do with leftovers from decorating 110 rooms? The Madonna Inn has the "What's Left" room, much of it in pink. PHYLLIS MADONNA

They were always expanding, and by 1962, the site included drive-through check-in or checkout, coffee shop, steakhouse, and bar. A popular photo op for those just visiting is the urinal in the men's room near the steakhouse, which features an eight-foot waterfall. Alex passed away in 2006, but Phyllis carries on, and their daughter and her husband continue to expand the operation, most recently with an expo center and a spa.

Themes have long been applied to the overall look of a hotel or motel. A couple vintage motels in Dallas, Texas, reflect the fascination with Spanish mission imagery. The Mission Motel, built in the early 1930s, features a pair of decorative bell towers. Next door is Alamo Plaza Hotel Courts, part of a chain founded in 1929 in Waco, Texas. Playing on the familiarity of the Alamo mission of San Antonio, it opened in more than two dozen locations, spreading as far as North Carolina, but only a few survive. The earliest, built in 1938 in Beaumont, Texas, is renamed Deluxe Inns and Suites. One in Baton Rouge, built in 1941, is called Alamo Plaza Motel. The one in Dallas, about the same age, retains its 1959 sign (the latter two lost theirs in recent years). Two more, built in 1948 in Houston and Atlanta, were both converted to housing. The Houston location is now apart-

The Alamo Plaza Motel of Baton Rouge, Louisiana, was once part of a lodging chain. DEBRA JANE SELTZER

ments, while the one in Atlanta is supportive housing for the homeless known as Santa Fe Villas.

Also once hugely popular were tepee-shaped rooms, most famously recalled in the Wigwam Village motels, started by Frank Redford in 1935.

His loosely franchised chain grew to seven locations, but only three remain—Kentucky, Arizona, and California—all independently operated. Cave City, Kentucky, with tepees in a semicircle, is the most rural. The tepees in Holbrook, Arizona, in a

The Chieftain Motel in Carrington, North Dakota, retains its Native American motif. MARK HUFSTETLER

U-shape, closed after original owner Chester E. Lewis died, but after a decade dormant, his children revived the place in 1989 and have parked vintage autos around the site. This and a site in Rialto, California, where the room layout is more random, are both along Old Route 66. Exciting news for roadside fans is that the Tee Pee Motel in Wharton, Texas, is being brought back to life. Opened in 1942, it had declined and closed, seeing life in recent decades only as a movie set for scenes in the 1995 remake of *Lolita*. New owners began the hard work of restoration of ten rooms and the neon sign in 2005.

Many other Native American–themed sites thrived and survive across the United States. As Earl Pomeroy noted in his 1957 book, *In Search of the Golden West: The Tourist in Western America*: "The Indian may be said to have arrived as a tourist attraction when a group of Colorado businessmen found it profitable in 1905 to build reproductions of parts of the Mesa Verde cliff

The Red Caboose Motel in Strasburg. SUSANNA DRAYNE

As a child of suburban Philadelphia, I fondly recall many summer vacations to the Neo-Colonial Carriage Stop Motel in Wildwood Crest, New Jersey. Every trip was marked by annual traditions, such as photos at or on the carriage, exciting night swims in the lighted pool, dressing up for dinner at places like Diamond Beach, and endless fun at the beach and Boardwalk. I haven't vacationed there since 1968, but I went back to the Wildwoods for the Society for Commercial Archeology conference in 1997. I was glad the motel was surviving, but I heard it was imminently threatened shortly thereafter. I'm thrilled to find it still in business.

—BETH L. SAVAGE, architectural historian for the National Register of Historic Places

Beth and her older sister Barbara at the hotel's carriage in 1967. BETH L. SAVAGE

in Carrington, North Dakota. The complex of motel, lounge, restaurant, and steakhouse was opened by Jud Tracy in 1964 and still features the numerous artifacts he collected, from buffalo robes to Navajo blankets to mannequins wearing complete outfits. It's been run since 1994 by his son Frank Klein and his wife, Lorie. Little has changed over the decades— even a tall Muffler Man–style Indian stands out front in a stereotypical "how" gesture—except that the Pow-Wow Lounge is now a sports bar, meaning the loss of a popular fluorescent mural that depicted the prairie at night.

More common, and continuing to open, are motels using railroad cabooses for the rooms. One of the best known is the Red Caboose Motel in Strasburg, Pennsylvania, with the Toy Train Museum, Choo Choo Barn, and Railroad Museum of Pennsylvania all nearby. It traces back to 1969, when Don Denlinger jokingly placed a bid on nineteen cabooses below scrap value but still won them. A new owner is working on restoring the forty-some cars, as they hadn't been updated since opening. Even older is the 1957 Caboose Motel in Avoca, New York, with five rooms offering queen beds plus upper and lower bunks in converted, restored red cabooses from 1916, set on rails laid in 1986. Caboose Junction Resort, southwest of Branson, Missouri, offers six refurbished 1920 Santa Fe railroad cabooses with twin sets of bunk beds and a queen bed in the cupola. It's situated on Table Rock Lake, with a boat dock for your own or rented pontoon, paddle, or fishing boat. At the Red Caboose Getaway near the Olympic Mountains in Washington, choose from the Casey Jones, with a conductor's desk and chair; the Orient Express, for luxury; the Circus Caboose; or a western-themed car. Then have breakfast in a restored 1937 Zephyr dining car. The newest is the Caboose Motel in Titusville, Pennsylvania, in the century-old oil region and not far from the Drake Well Museum, with twenty-one cabooses next to the town's Perry Street Station.

dwellings near Manitou. . . . Tourists were not quite ready to leave the main lines of travel to go to the Indian, but he had achieved a negotiable value as decoration." Though some of the sites are seen today as derogatory, many have adapted by telling the Native American side of their local history. One such survivor is the Chieftain Motel

Besides all the caboose motels, the Chattanooga Choo Choo in Tennessee features forty-

The Sleepy Hollow in the middle of Green River, Utah, competes with franchises clustered at the interstate exits at each end of town. The sign conjures more soothing images of rest than the name might suggest.

eight Victorian sleeping cars for accommodations. The twenty-four-acre complex also includes Terminal Station, dedicated in 1909, closed in 1970, but reopened a few years later for dining and shopping. Not far away, Union Station offers accommodations in the landmark Romanesque-style building. It reflected the glamour of rail travel at the time, with barrel-vaulted ceiling, Tiffany stained glass, two alligator ponds, and a bronze likeness of Mercury atop a clock tower. Opened in 1900 and closed in the 1970s, it's been reborn as an upscale hotel with 125 rooms.

As mid-twentieth-century hotels and motels close and are demolished, appreciation for them is growing. In Austin, Texas, the upscale Hotel San Jose opened in 1936 as the Spanish Colonial–style San Jose Court, and old postcards show tidy rooms behind creamy stucco walls with red tile roofs. It advertised itself as an "ultra modern tourist court," but that was nothing compared with today's hip, urban bungalow-style remodel, which, as one reviewer writes, feels "both retro and thoroughly up-to-the-minute." In Scottsdale, Arizona, the Hotel Valley Ho has likewise been reborn for a new young crowd. In 1956, it was Scottsdale's first year-round resort, and it became a playground for stars, including Tony Curtis and Janet Leigh and Robert Wagner and Natalie Wood, who married here in 1957. After decades of decline, an $80 million renovation has merged its midcentury lounge chic with modern conveniences, including a Trader Vic's Polynesian restaurant. The hundreds of Art Deco motels in and near Miami Beach followed the same path, from popular to run-down to once again cool. Beachfront prices can be pretty high, but lots of small motels a few blocks back, or later motels to the north, still offer affordable, time-warp accommodations.

Many of the mom-and-pop midcentury motels have been converted to low-rent housing, abandoned, or bulldozed. Midcentury guidebooks

Above: The big sign for the Rocket Motel in Custer, South Dakota, lights up the night.

Left: Gregory Smith snapped young Harrison during the Society for Commercial Archeology's tour of Seattle roadside landmarks. The Klose-In Motel, opened in 1920, is one of a number of mom-and-pop survivors along Aurora Avenue. As with most cities, this former main drag has been in decline for decades, but vintage businesses can be found still sporting vibrant neon. This sign rejects any thought of parallel lines. SUZANNE WRAY

such as *Establishing and Operating a Year-Round Motor Court*, by the U.S. Department of Commerce, made future possibilities look limitless. No one foresaw the overwhelming changes wrought by interstates and franchises. The survivors that still sport clean rooms and neon signs are gaining a following among those who like to travel old highways. Places like the Klose-In in Seattle, Washington, the Rocket Motel in Custer, South Dakota, or hundreds of other small motels still draw budget travelers, bikers, and foreign tourists who are looking for convenience, friendly service, and low rates.

SPOTLIGHT ON
Tourist Cabins

Tourist cabins, once so pervasive, are mostly relegated to natural resort areas. Often they have a log cabin theme, like a pair of motels about six miles north of Asheville, North Carolina. Both the Log Cabin Motor Court and The Pines Cottages retain their AAA ratings, a key element for survival these days, when travelers want no surprises at the end of their day. The Log Cabin opened in 1931; its claim to fame is that Robert Mitchum used the Gold View cabin as a dressing room during the filming of *Thunder Road* in the late 1950s. All eighteen cabins have names like Kozy Korner and Snuggle Inn. Inside are paneling and trim in various woods or exposed beams. At The Pines, opened in 1932, there are two cabins and thirteen cottages, many with knotty pine paneling.

Since their peak in the 1920s and 1930s, vintage tourist cabins have been torn down, joined to form strips of motel rooms, or moved and converted into storage sheds and playhouses. More recently, some folk are realizing the nostalgic appeal of the tiny homes away from home. The lack of a phone, Wi-Fi, or cable television may turn off some, but it is quite

Cabins are reserved months in advance at Badlands National Park, South Dakota

appealing to those who've had enough of calls, e-mail, and reality TV.

Compare these vivid descriptions by Zephine Humphrey in *Green Mountains to Sierras* (1936). At Rawlins, Wyoming, she and her husband found what she described as "the crudest cabin we had yet occupied. No running water (which was just as well, for it would

The cabins at Sears Motel in East Glacier Park, Montana. MARK HUFSTETLER

Mac's tepee-shaped cabins, built in 1934, recently closed in Cherokee, North Carolina.

surely have frozen), the minimum of furniture (which was also just as well, for the room was two by four), no 'conveniences' of any kind except in a communal bath house. A gas stove, however, and a fairly comfortable bed."

In contrast, she praised a camp in Ogden, Utah: "One of the best, perhaps the very best, we had found anywhere: with seven (yes, seven; count them yourself!) electric lights, with two gas stoves, and a porcelain sink, and a complete kitchen equipment. All the woodwork

The cabins look cozy at Hearthside Village in Bethlehem, New Hampshire. STEVE HUGGINS

and furniture had been freshly painted, and there was a new linoleum rug on the floor. Also a patchwork quilt on the bed."

Some, like the cabins at Cedar Pass Lodge in Badlands National Park, South Dakota, are modern but retain a hint of their roots, such as those built in 1928 with no in-room phones. The Nancy Lincoln Inn, a privately owned gift shop and mini-museum in Hodgenville, Kentucky, beside the Abraham Lincoln Birthplace National Historic Site, was built of chestnut logs and red heart pine in 1928. In 2005, the builder's grandson, Carl Howell Jr., restored the cabins to original condition. They are air-conditioned but have no phones or indoor plumbing, though a modern bathhouse is nearby.

The Sears Motel and Campground in East Glacier Park, Montana, has sixteen rooms plus RV spaces, a convenience store, and a gift shop with "Almost a Million Shirts in Stock," all located within a nine-hole golf course.

For classic early auto-era cabins, Hearthside Village in Bethlehem, New Hampshire, features sixteen tiny gabled cottages built between 1938 and 1946 by Arthur and Rose Plante. New owners bought it in 1982 and renamed it. Testifying to its popularity, the cabins are sometimes fully booked a year in advance.

GETTING THERE

Afton Station
Old Route 66
Afton, Oklahoma
www.PostcardsFromTheRoad.net

Alamo Plaza Efficiency Apartments
4343 Old Spanish Trail
Just west of MacGregor Park
Houston, Texas

Alamo Plaza Hotel Courts
712 Fort Worth Ave.
I-30, exit to Sylvan Ave. via Dallas–Fort
   Worth Turnpike
Dallas, Texas

Alamo Plaza Motel
4243 Florida Blvd.
I-110, follow Florida east
Baton Rouge, Louisiana

Alamo Village
Off U.S. 90 on FM 674, 7 miles north of
   town (120 miles west of San Antonio)
Brackettville, Texas
www.alamovillage.com

Alligator Adventure
U.S. 17 at Barefoot Landing
North Myrtle Beach, South Carolina
www.alligatoradventure.com

Allison's Mini Golf
5456 Lake Rd.
Geneva-on-the-Lake, Ohio

Andy's Frozen Custard
2119 N. Glenstone Ave.
Springfield, Missouri
www.eatandys.com

Angel's Diner
209 Reid St.
Palatka, Florida

Arcade Amusements
930 block of Manitou Ave. stretching
   to Park Ave
Manitou Springs, Colorado

Arizona Girls Candles
200 Main St.
Oatman, Arizona

Arne's Royal Hawaiian Hotel
200 W. Baker Blvd.
Off I-15, CA-127/Death Valley Rd. exit
Baker, California

Astroland
1000 Surf Ave. between W. 10th St.
   and Jones Walk
Brooklyn, New York
www.astroland.com

BRING YOUR CAMERA...

Since 1965, and still in the same family, the Aut-O-Rama has cozied up to the ramps of Ohio Turnpike exit 152 southwest of Cleveland. It was twinned in 1972.

Aut-O-Rama Twin Drive-In
33395 Lorain Rd./OH 10
Just west of Ohio Turnpike exit 152
North Ridgeville, Ohio
www.autoramadrivein.com

Ave Maria Grotto
1600 Saint Bernard Dr. SE
East of town near U.S. 278
Cullman, Alabama
www.avemariagrotto.com

Bar-B-Q Ranch
3311 N. Valley Pike/U.S. 11
I-81, Exit 251 and just south
Harrisonburg, Virginia

Bedrock City
U.S. 16 & U.S. 385
Custer, South Dakota
www.flintstonesbedrockcity.com

Bengies Drive-In Theatre
3417 Eastern Blvd./MD 150
East of downtown Baltimore, just east
  of Martin State Airport
Baltimore, Maryland
www.bengies.com

Bennett's Pit Bar-B-Que and KJ's Saloon
714 River Rd.
At U.S. 441, traffic light 5
Gatlinburg, Tennessee
www.bennetts-bbq.com

Best Value Inn Villa Motel
481 Manitou Ave.
Manitou Springs, Colorado
www.villamotel.com

Best Western Pavilions
(former Space Age Lodge)
1176 W. Katella Ave.
Anaheim, California

Best Western Route 66 Rail Haven
203 S. Glenstone Ave.
Springfield, Missouri
www.route66railhaven.com

Best Western—Space Age Lodge
401 E. Pima St./AZ 85
I-8, Exit 115
Gila Bend, Arizona
www.bestwesternspaceagelodge.com

Big Chicken
12 Cobb Pkwy. NE/U.S. 41
At Roswell St./GA 120, just south of
  American Amusement Park
I-75, Exit 263 or 265
Marietta, Georgia
www.bigchickenchorus.org/BigChicken
  Landmark.html

The Big Duck
61 Bellows Pond Rd.
Just off Flanders Rd./NY 24
Flanders, New York

Big Mike's Rock and Gift Shop and
  Mystery House
566 Old Mammoth Cave Rd.
Take I-65, Exit 53
Cave City, Kentucky
www.mammothcave.com/big_mikes.htm

The Big Pig
Pig Stand restaurant
801 S. Presa St.
San Antonio, Texas

Big Texan
7701 I-40 East, Exit 75
Amarillo, Texas
www.bigtexan.com

The Bigfoot Motel
CA 299 at CA 96/Bigfoot Scenic Highway
Willow Creek, California
www.bigfootmotel.com

Blue Swallow Motel
815 E. Route 66 Blvd.
Tucumcari, New Mexico
www.blueswallowmotel.com

The Blue Whale
2705 N. Highway 66
Just north of I-44, Exit 240, and northeast
    of Tulsa
Catoosa, Oklahoma

Bozo's Hot Pit Bar-B-Que
342 U.S. 70
Mason, Tennessee

Broncos Drive-In
4540 Leavenworth
Omaha, Nebraska

Bug Ranch at Longhorn Trading Post
I-40, Exit 96, south side
Conway, Texas

Dun Boy Restaurant and World's Largest
    Thermometer
72139 Baker Blvd.
I-15, Exit 246
Baker, California

Cabazon Dinosaurs
50800 Seminole Dr.
I-10, Main Street exit, 13 miles west
    of Palm Springs
Cabazon, California
www.cabazondinosaurs.com

Caboose Junction Resort
162 Caboose Lane
South of I-44 and Silver Dollar City
Lampe, Missouri
www.caboosejunctionresort.com

Caboose Motel
8620 NY 415
North of the intersection of I-86 (Southern
    Tier Expy.) and I-390 (Genesee Expy.)
Avoca, New York
www.caboosemotel.net

The Caboose Motel
407 S. Perry St.
Titusville, Pennsylvania
www.octrr.org/caboosemotel.htm

Cadillac Ranch
Old Route 66/I-40
A few miles west of town, exit to Arnot Rd.
    and drive east
Amarillo, Texas
www.libertysoftware.be/cml/cadillacranch/
    crmain.htm

Campbell Bros. Confusion Hill
75001 N. U.S. 101
Piercy, California
www.confusionhill.com

Canyon Trading Post
5171 N. AZ 64
Williams, Arizona

Carhenge
2141 C.R. 59/NE 87
2¹/₂ miles north of town in open fields
Alliance, Nebraska
www.carhenge.com

Caribbean Motel
5600 Ocean Ave.
At Buttercup Rd.
Wildwood Crest, New Jersey
www.caribbeanmotel.com

Carriage Stop Motel
8200 Atlantic Ave. at St. Paul Ave.
Wildwood Crest, New Jersey
www.carriagestopmotel.com

Casa Bonita
6715 W. Colfax Ave./U.S. 40
Just south of I-70 between Wadsworth Blvd.
    and Sheridan Blvd.
Denver, Colorado
www.casabonitadenver.com

Cattlemen's Steakhouse
1309 S. Agnew
In Stockyards City just south of I-40
Oklahoma City, Oklahoma
www.cattlemensrestaurant.com

Cedar Pass Lodge
20681 SD 240/Badlands Loop Rd.
I-90, Exit 131, go 8 miles south to just past
    the park visitor center
Interior, South Dakota
www.nps.gov/badl
www.cedarpasslodge.com

Chattanooga Choo Choo Holiday Inn
1400 Market St.
Chattanooga, Tennessee
www.choochoo.com

Cheese Haven
2920 E. Harbor Rd./OH 163 at OH 53
4 miles east of Port Clinton
Marblehead, Ohio
www.cheesehaven.com

Cherry Pie and Pan
6591 U.S. 31 S.
Charlevoix, Michigan

Chick-Inn Drive-In
501 Holmes Rd. at Prospect
Ypsilanti, Michigan

Chief Yellowhorse Trading Post
AZ 66 and AZ 118
I-40, Exit 359
Lupton, Arizona

Chieftain Motel
60 Fourth Ave. S.
Intersection of ND 200 and U.S. 281
Carrington, North Dakota
www.chieftainmotel.com

Christ of the Ozarks statue
U.S. 62 W.
3 miles west of town
Eureka Springs, Missouri

Cielito Lindo
730 N. Glenstone Ave.
Springfield, Missouri

Circus Hall of Fame
3076 E. Circus Lane
Between Fort Wayne and Indianapolis
    along IN 124
Peru, Indiana
www.circushalloffame.com

Clark's Trading Post
U.S. 3
North Woodstock, New Hampshire
www.clarkstradingpost.com

The Cliff House at Pikes Peak
306 Cañon Ave.
Manitou Springs, Colorado
www.thecliffhouse.com

Clifton's Cafeteria Brookdale
648 S. Broadway, at 7th St.
Los Angeles, California
www.cliftonscafeteria.com

Coffee Pot
Bedford County Fairgrounds
Bus. U.S. 30 W.
Bedford, Pennsylvania

Coney Island
6201 Kellogg Ave.
Cincinnati, Ohio
www.coneyislandpark.com

Coney Island Museum and Sideshows
    by the Seashore
1208 Surf Ave. (at W. 12th St.)
Brooklyn, New York
www.coneyisland.com/sideshow.shtml

Conneaut Lake Park USA
12382 Center St./PA 618
I-79, Exit 147B
Conneaut Lake, Pennsylvania
www.conneautlakepark.com

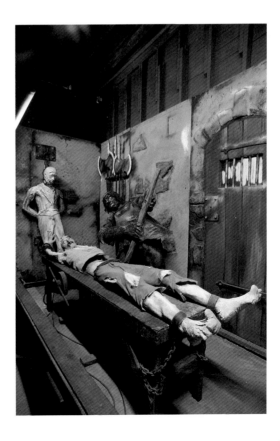

Members of Darkride and Funhouse Enthusiasts helped restore the Fright Zone at Erieview. It began life in the 1960s at West View Park, north of Pittsburgh. After being auctioned in 2006, it's been moved back to western Pennsylvania to Conneaut Lake Park. It contains scenes created by one of the great dark attraction artists, the late Bill Tracy, and is the last permanent surviving ride system made by the Herschell company.
RICK DAVIS

123

This 1926 Mobil station at Cool Springs, west of Kingman, Arizona, was almost completely destroyed but has been rebuilt and now sells souvenirs.

Cool Springs Museum/Gift Shop
8275 Oatman Highway
Kingman, Arizona
www.coolspringsroute66.com

Coral Castle
28655 South Dixie Highway/U.S. 1
Florida Turnpike, Exit 5
Homestead, Florida
www.coralcastle.com

Corn Palace
604 N. Main St.
Mitchell, South Dakota
www.cornpalace.org/newpages/palace.html

Country Dove Gifts and Tea Room
610 W. Third St.
Elk City, Oklahoma

Craig's Bar-B-Q/Craig Brothers Café
U.S. 70 W./W. Walnut
Between Memphis and Little Rock
DeValls Bluff, Arkansas

Crowne Plaza Quaker Square
135 S. Broadway
I-77 to Exit 22A and go south on Broadway
    just over a mile
Akron, Ohio
www.quakersquare.com

Cypress Gardens
6000 Cypress Gardens Blvd./FL 540
Southwest of Orlando, from I-4, take U.S. 27 S.
Winter Haven, Florida
www.cypressgardens.com

DelGrosso's Amusement Park
Bus. U.S. 220, between I-99 Exits 41 and 45
Tipton, Pennsylvania
www.delgrossos.com/dap.html

Del's Headquarters
1260 Oaklawn Ave.
Cranston, Rhode Island
www.dels.com

Deluxe Inns and Suites
1930 College St./U.S. 90
East from I-10
Beaumont, Texas

Deno's Wonder Wheel Amusement Park
3059 W. 12th St.
Denos Vourderis Place
Brooklyn, New York
www.wonderwheel.com

Desert Inn and Restaurant
5570 S. Kenansville Rd.
YeeHaw Junction, Florida
www.desertinnrestaurant.com

Dinosaur Gardens
11160 U.S. 23 S.
Ossineke, Michigan
www.dinosaurgardensllc.com

Dinosaur Land
3848 Stonewall Jackson Highway
Between Winchester and Front Royal
    at the intersection of U.S. 522, U.S. 340,
    and VA 277
White Post, Virginia
www.dinosaurland.com

Dinosaur Park
Skyline Dr.
Rapid City, South Dakota
www.rapidcitycvb.com

Dinosaur World
5145 Harvey Tew Rd.
I-4, Exit 17, east of Tampa
Plant City, Florida
www.dinoworld.net

Dinosaur World
711 Mammothcave Rd.
I-65 Exit 53, between Nashville
   and Louisville
Cave City, Kentucky
www.dinoworld.net

Dinotown Jurassic Theme Park
53480 Bridal Falls Rd.
Rosedale, British Columbia, Canada
www.dinotown.com

Dog Bark Park Inn Bed and Breakfast
U.S. 95
Cottonwood, Idaho
www.dogbarkparkinn.com

Donut Drive-In
6525 Chippewa St.
Along the later Route 66 at Watson Road
St. Louis, Missouri

Doo Wop Preservation League
3201 Pacific Ave.
Wildwood, New Jersey
www.doowopusa.org

Eartha at DeLorme
2 DeLorme Dr.
Yarmouth, Maine
www.delorme.com

East Potomac Golf Course
972 Ohio Dr. SW
East Potomac Park
Washington, D.C.

Eddie's Grill
5377 Lake Rd. E.
Geneva-on-the-Lake, Ohio

Eisler Brothers Old Riverton Store
7109 SE Highway 66
Riverton, Kansas
www.eislerbros.com

El Colorado Lodge
23 Manitou Ave.
Manitou Springs, Colorado
www.elcolorado.pikes-peak.com

El Rancho Hotel and Motel
1000 E. 66 Ave.
Gallup, New Mexico
www.elranchohotel.com

Enchanted Forest/Water Safari
3183 NY 28
Old Forge, New York
www.watersafari.com

Escape from Dinosaur Kingdom
U.S. 11
Natural Bridge, Virginia
www.naturalbridgeva.com/dinoking.html

Exotic Animal Paradise
I-44, Exit 88
Strafford, Missouri

Extreme World
1800 Wisconsin Dells Parkway
Wisconsin Dells, Wisconsin
www.extremeworld.com

F.A.S.T (Fiberglass Animals Shapes
   and Trademarks)
14177 County Highway Q
Sparta, Wisconsin
www.fastkorp.com

Fairlee Drive-In and Motel
1809 U.S. 5 N.
Off I-91
Fairlee, Vermont

Family Pie Shop
U.S. 70 W./W. Walnut
DeValls Bluff, Arkansas

Fat Boy Drive-In
111 Bath Rd.
Brunswick, Maine

Fields of the Wood Bible Park
10000 NC 294
West of Chattanooga, Tennessee, 10 miles
    north of U.S. 64/74
Murphy, North Carolina
www.fieldsofthewoodbiblepark.com

Flintstones Bedrock City
U.S. 180 at AZ 64 north of Williams
Valle, Arizona

Foamhenge
U.S. 11 N.
Natural Bridge, Virginia

Former Airway Drive-In
10634 St. Charles Rock Rd.
Saint Ann, Missouri

Fort Cody Trading Post
101 Halligan Dr.
U.S. 83 at I-80 Exit 177
North Platte, Nebraska
www.fortcody.com

The Fort Restaurant
19192 CO 8
I-70, Exit 260, just north of U.S. 285
Morrison, Colorado
www.thefort.com

Franks Diner
508 58th St.
Kenosha, Wisconsin

Friends of the Watts Towers Arts Center
1727 E. 107th St.
Los Angeles, California
www.wattstowers.org

Frontier Village
Buffalo Museum and Gift Shop
500 17th St. SE
Jamestown, North Dakota
www.buffalomuseum.com/frontier.htm

Fruit and Spice Park
24801 SW 187th Ave.
Homestead, Florida
www.fruitandspice.org

Funk's Grove
5257 Old Route 66
Shirley, Illinois
www.funkspuremaplesirup.com

Garden of Eden
305 E. Second St.
Lucas, Kansas
www.garden-of-eden-lucas-kansas.com

Garden of the Gods Trading Post
324 Beckers Lane
U.S. 24 to Garden of the Gods Road
    and follow signs
Manitou Springs, Colorado
www.co-trading-post.com/tp_html/gar-hist.htm

Garden of the Gods Visitor and Nature Center
1805 N. 30th Street at Gateway Rd.
Just north of Manitou Springs and U.S. 24
Colorado Springs, Colorado
www.gardenofgods.com

Gatorama
6180 U.S. 27
Just west of Lake Okeechobee
Palmdale, Florida
www.gatorama.com

Gatorland
14501 S. Orange Blossom Trail (FL 441)
South Orlando, Florida
Just north of the Orlando-Kissimmee line near
    the intersection of I-4 and toll road 417
www.gatorland.com

The Gay Dolphin
916 N. Ocean Blvd.
Myrtle Beach, South Carolina
www.gaydolphin.com

Ghost Town in the Sky park
890 Soco Rd.
Maggie Valley, North Carolina
www.ghosttowninthesky.com

Giant's Camp restaurant
9816 U.S. 41 S.
Gibsonton, Florida

Gibtown Showman's Club
International Independent Showman's
    Association
6915 Riverview Dr.
Gibsontown, Florida

Gnome on the Range Mini Golf
Kelder's Farm and U-Pick
5678 Route 209, west of I-87
Kerhokson, New York
www.hoeplo.org

Grasshopper Junction
U.S. 93
About 15 miles north of Kingman
Grasshopper Junction, Arizona

Gravity Hill
From U.S. 30 in Schellsburg, turn north
    on PA 96 and follow the signs
New Paris, Pennsylvania
www.gravityhill.com

Great Smoky Mountains National Park
Spanning Tennessee and North Carolina
107 Park Headquarters Rd.
Gatlinburg, Tennessee
www.nps.gov/grsm

Guidestones
Just east of Hartwell Highway/GA 77
Elberton, Georgia
www.tylwytheg.com/guide.html

Haines Shoe House
Shoe House Rd., north of PA 462
Hallam, Pennsylvania

Hard Rock Park
U.S. 501 at the Intracoastal Waterway
Myrtle Beach, South Carolina
www.hrpusa.com
Opening in 2008

Harland Sanders Café and Museum
688 U.S. 25 W.
I-75, Exit 29
Corbin, Kentucky

Harman's Café
3890 S. State St.
Salt Lake City, Utah

Harpersville Drive-In
45 Woodland Rd./CR 475
Along U.S. 280
Harpersville, Alabama

Haunted Mansion
112 Broadway
Wisconsin Dells, Wisconsin

Hawaiian Rumble
3210 U.S. 17 S.
North Myrtle Beach, South Carolina
www.prominigolf.com/rumble.html

Hearthside Village Cottage Motel
1267 Main St./U.S. 302
1 mile east of I-93, Exit 40
Bethlehem, New Hampshire
www.hearthsidevillage.com

Highway Garage
Portola Ave. at N. L St.
Livermore, California

Historic Apple Valley Roadside Attraction
9351 U.S. 68 W.
Just south of Paducah
Sharpe, Kentucky

Hoffman's Playland
608 Loudon Rd./U.S. 9
1 mile south of Latham Traffic Circle
Latham, New York
www.hoffmansplayland.com

BRING YOUR CAMERA!

Hole N' The Rock
11037 S. U.S. 191
12 miles south of town
Moab, Utah
www.holentherock.com

Holiday World and Splashin' Safari
452 E. Christmas Blvd./IN 162
    and IN 245
From I-64, take Exit 57 or 63
Santa Claus, Indiana
www.holidayworld.com

Hotel San Jose
1316 S. Congress Ave.
1/2 mile south of downtown
Austin, Texas
www.sanjosehotel.com

The Hotel Valley Ho
6850 E. Main St.
Scottsdale, Arizona
www.historichotels.org/hotel/285

Idlewild park
U.S. 30 E.
Ligonier, Pennsylvania
www.idlewild.com

Igloo City
George Parks Highway/AK 3
Between Anchorage and Fairbanks
Near Cantwell, Alaska

Igloo Ice Cream
4131 Monroe St.
I-475, Douglas Rd. exit
Toledo, Ohio

International Marketplace
2330 Kalakaua Ave.
Waikiki, Oahu, Hawaii
www.internationalmarketplacewaikiki.com

Jackalope
3rd and Center Streets, SW corner
Jackalope Square at Bolln Memorial Park
Douglas, Wyoming
www.jackalope.org

Jenkinson's Boardwalk
300 Ocean Ave.
Point Pleasant Beach, New Jersey
www.jenkinsons.com

Jungle Adventures
2703 Lee Highway/U.S. 11
Off I-81 Exit 5
Bristol, Virginia
www.jungleadventures.net

The Streamlined Moderne Jones Motor Company on Central Avenue in Albuquerque served as a Ford dealer, gas station, and repair shop from 1939 to 1957. After other uses, it sat closed until 2000, when Kelly's Brewery converted it into a restaurant and brewpub. The garage doors were preserved and vintage pumps were added.

Jungle Adventures
26205 FL 50 E.
17 miles east of Orlando
Christmas, Florida
www.jungleadventures.com

KFC Colonel logo
Groom Rd. at Old Mill St.
About 25 miles SW of U.S. 6
Rachel, Nevada

K-N Root Beer
30000 Olsen Blvd.
Amarillo, Texas

Kalahari Resort Waterparks
1305 Kalahari Drive
Wisconsin Dells, Wisconsin
www.kalahariresorts.com

Kelly's Brewery
(former Jones Motor Company)
3226 Central SE
Albuquerque, New Mexico
www.kellysbrewpub.com

Kennywood park
4800 Kennywood Blvd.
West Mifflin, Pennsylvania
www.kennywood.com

Kiddie Park
215 N. Cherokee Ave. at Hensley Blvd.
In Johnstone Park, six blocks north of U.S. 60
Bartlesville, Oklahoma
www.kiddiepark.net

Kiddie Park
3015 Broadway
San Antonio, Texas
www.kiddiepark.com

King's Chef
110 E. Costilla St.
Colorado Springs, Colorado
www.kingschefdiner.com

Klose-In Motel
9309 Aurora Ave. N. Highway 99
Seattle, Washington

Lakeside Park's beautiful Art Deco Cyclone has warnings that you're in for a wild ride. Brian's cracked rib confirmed that.

Knoebels Amusement Resort
Off route 487
I-80 Exit 224, take PA 54 east
   to PA 487 and go north
Elysburg, Pennsylvania
www.knoebels.com

Kon Tiki Restaurant and Lounge
4625 E. Broadway Blvd.
Tucson, Arizona
www.kontiki-tucson.com

La Casa
4432 Leavenworth
Omaha, Nebraska

Lakemont Park
700 Park Ave.
Altoona, Pennsylvania
www.lakemontparkfun.com

Lakeside Amusement Park
4601 Sheridan Blvd.
Just south of I-70 Exits 270 and 271A
Denver, Colorado
www.lakesideamusementpark.com

Land of Oz
Wylie Park, 1 mile north on U.S. 281
Aberdeen, South Dakota
www.aberdeencvb.com/storybook.html

Launching Pad Café
810 E. Baltimore St./U.S. 53
Wilmington, Illinois
www.launchingpadroute66.com

Leaning Tower of Niles
6300 W. Touhy Ave.
Just east of N. California Ave./U.S. 14
Niles, Illinois

Legs of Ozymandias
I-27 and Sundown Lane
Between Amarillo and Canyon, Texas

Log Cabin Motor Court
330 Weaverville Highway
Asheville, North Carolina
www.cabinlodging.com

The Loony Bin
633 Wisconsin Dells Parkway
Wisconsin Dells, Wisconsin

Louis' Lunch
263 Crown St.
Between College St. and High St.
New Haven, Connecticut
www.louislunch.com

Mac's Indian Village
160 Teepee Dr.
Just south of U.S. 441/Bus. 441
    intersection
Cherokee, North Carolina

Madonna Inn
100 Madonna Rd.
U.S. 101, Madonna Rd. exit
San Luis Obispo, California
www.madonnainn.com

Madsen Donuts
5426 Lake Rd. E.
Geneva-on-the-Lake, Ohio

Mai-Kai Restaurant
3599 N. Federal Highway/U.S. 1
I-95, Oakland Park Blvd. exit
Fort Lauderdale, Florida
www.maikai.com

Maid Rite Sandwich Shop
(with Wall of Gum)
125 N. Broadway St.
Greenville, Ohio

Manitou and Pike's Peak Cog Railway
515 Ruxton Ave.
Manitou Springs, Colorado
www.cograilway.com

Marsh's Free Museum
409 S. Pacific Ave.
Long Beach, Washington
www.marshsfreemuseum.com

Mayday Golf
715 U.S. 17 N.
North Myrtle Beach, South Carolina
www.maydaygolf.com

Medieval Times Dinner and Tournament
Buena Park, California
Toronto, Canada
Kissimmee, Florida
Lawrenceville, Georgia
Schaumburg, Illinois
Hanover, Maryland
Lyndhurst, New Jersey
Myrtle Beach, South Carolina
Dallas, Texas
www.medievaltimes.com

Mel-Haven Lodge
3715 W. Colorado Ave./U.S. Bus. 24 W.
Colorado Springs, Colorado
www.melhavenlodge.pikes-peak.com

Melinda Court
2400 W. College St.
Springfield, Missouri

Memphis Championship Miniature
   Golf Course
Memphis Kiddie Park
10340 Memphis Ave.
Brooklyn, Ohio
www.memphiskiddiepark.com

Memphis Drive-In Theater website
Formerly in Brooklyn, Ohio
www.memphisdrivein.com

MidPoint Café and Gift Shop
Old Route 66 West
Exit 22 from I-40 E. or Exit 23A from I-40 W.
Adrian, Texas
www.uglycrustpies.com

Mike Bjorn's Fine Clothing and Museum
5614 6th Ave.
Kenosha, Wisconsin
www.tux-a-rama.com

Million Dollar Cowboy Bar
25 N. Cache St.
Jackson, Wyoming
www.milliondollarcowboybar.com

Mission Motel
514 W. Commerce St.
Dallas, Texas

Monkey Jungle
14805 SW 216th St. (Hainlin Mill Rd.)
   near SW 147th Ave.
Just off U.S. 1 in South Dade
Miami, Florida
www.monkeyjungle.com

An airplane looms above the links at Mayday Golf in Myrtle Beach, South Carolina.

Monterey Non-Smokers Motel
2402 Central Ave. SW/Old Route 66
Albuquerque, New Mexico
www.nonsmokersmotel.com

Moody's Diner
U.S. 1
Waldoboro, Maine
www.moodysdiner.com

Mount Atlanticus Minotaur Goff
707 N. Kings Highway
Myrtle Beach, South Carolina
www.mtatlanticus.com

Mt. Olympus Water and Theme Park
1881 Wisconsin Dells Parkway
Wisconsin Dells, Wisconsin
www.mtolympusthemepark.com

Mountain Mist Ice Cream
Route 86
Saranac Lake, New York

Munger Moss Motel
1336 E. Route 66
Lebanon, Missouri
www.mungermoss.com

Musee Mecanique
Pier 45, Shed A at the end of Taylor St.
Fisherman's Wharf
San Francisco, California
www.museemechanique.org

Museum of Historic Torture Devices
740 Eddy St.
Wisconsin Dells, Wisconsin
www.dellstorturemuseum.com

Mystery Spot
465 Mystery Spot Rd.
From CA 1, take the Ocean St. exit
Santa Cruz, California
www.mysteryspot.com

Nancy Lincoln Inn
2975 Lincoln Farm Rd.
Off U.S. 31 E. at Nancy Lincoln Inn Rd.
Just south of the Abraham Lincoln Birthplace
    National Historic Site
Hodgenville, Kentucky
www.nancylincolninn.com

Naples Zoo at Caribbean Gardens
1590 Goodlette Rd.
Naples, Florida
www.napleszoo.com

Nathan's Famous
1310 Surf Ave.
Brooklyn, New York
www.nathansfamous.com

Nellie Bly Park (temporarily closed)
1824 Shore Parkway
B6 bus stops in front of park
Brooklyn, New York

Nibbles Woodaway
New England Pest Control
161 O'Connell St.
See it from I-95 or take Exit 19
Providence, Rhode Island
www.bluebug.com

Noah's Ark Waterpark
1410 Wisconsin Dells Parkway
Wisconsin Dells, Wisconsin
www.noahsarkwaterpark.com

Old Spanish Sugar Mill Grill
    and Griddle House
FL 17 N.
DeLeon Springs, Florida

One Log House Espresso and Gifts
705 U.S. 101
Near Richardson Grove State Park
Garberville, California
www.one-loghouse.com

Orange Show Center for Visionary Art
2402 Munger St.
Houston, Texas
www.orangeshow.org

The giant oranges of the California roadside are my totem, my measure of all architecture. They entered my imagination at an early age, framed in the passenger window of our Mercury station wagon as our vacationing family drove Highway 99 between Oakland and Los Angeles. Eager to make time, my father never actually allowed us to stop at a giant orange stand, but years later, when I was becoming an architect, those briefly glimpsed images rose again in my mind's eye. Architecture, they said, is far more than steel and glass, than utility and structure.

What were these giant oranges? Where did they come from? Were they some gigantic species, growing fat and fantastic in the fertile soil of the San Joaquin Valley? Could be. Or were these oranges normal size and the rest of the world had shrunken to microscopic size? Had we entered the Valley of the Giants? Had the verities of scale and proportion become elastic? Could be. The myths and realities of California have always been hard to separate.

Or were these structures simply heartfelt monuments, elegant, simple, and profound reminders of the great citrus orchards that flourished historically in California's southern valleys? Their perfect spheres expressed a timeless grandeur; their dimpled surfaces evoked a sensuous tactility that anyone who has ever peeled a succulent orange could understand.

Clearly these oranges were not simple one-line jokes, good for a laugh and then forgotten. They resonated with mysteries and questions about the nature of reality. In later years, I stopped and got out and examined these oranges. Some were plaster on wood frames; some had metal peels bolted together longitudinally. They were commercial buildings intended to sell juice and hamburgers. But they would not let me forget that architecture was much more than a physical structure. I have never forgotten.

—ALAN HESS, author of *Googie Redux: Ultramodern Roadside Architecture*

FAN FAVORITE

Orange World
5395 W. Irlo Bronson Highway/U.S. 192
2 1/2 miles east of Disney World
Kissimmee, Florida
www.orangeworld192.com

Oregon Vortex and House of Mystery
4303 Sardine Creek Rd.
I-5 between Exits 40 and 43
Gold Hill, Oregon
www.oregonvortex.com

O'Rourke's Diner
728 Main St.
Middletown, Connecticut

Ozarkland
3233 C.R. 211
I-70, Exit 148, U.S. 54
Kingdom City, Missouri

Page Museum at the La Brea Tar Pits
5801 Wilshire Blvd.
North of I-10, west of I-110
Los Angeles, California
www.tarpits.org

Painted Desert Trading Post
I-40, Exit 320, follow rough road north,
   then west
East of Holbrook, Arizona

Palace Diner
Franklin St., just off U.S. 1
Biddeford, Maine

Paradise Gardens
84 Knox St.
Two blocks off U.S. 27
Summerville, Georgia
www.finster.com/ParadiseGardens.htm
www.finstersparadisegardens.org

Parkette Drive-In
1216 New Circle Rd. NE
Lexington, Kentucky

Par-King Skill Golf
21711 Milwaukee Ave.
Near Aptakisic Rd.
Lincolnshire, Illinois
www.par-king.com

Parrot Jungle
1111 Parrot Jungle Trail
Between downtown Miami and South Beach,
    off MacArthur Causeway/I-395
Miami, Florida
www.parrotjungle.com

Paul Bunyan Land at This Old Farm
    Pioneer Village
17553 MN 18, 7 miles east of town
Brainerd, Minnesota
www.thisoldfarm.net

Paul Bunyan Logging Camp Museum
1110 Carson Park Dr.
Eau Clair, Wisconsin
www.paulbunyancamp.org

Paul Bunyan's Flashlight/Water Tower
Bus. MN 371/S. 6th St. at MN 210/Washington St.
Brainerd, Minnesota

Perry's Nut House
45 Searsport Ave./U.S. 1
Belfast, Maine
www.perrysnuthouse.com

Petrified Wood Park
500 Main St.
Five blocks north of U.S. 12
Lemmon, South Dakota
www.lemmonsd.com/petrefied.html

Phillips 66 station (restored)
W. First St.
McLean, Texas

Pike's Peak Cog Railway
515 Ruxton Ave.
Off Manitou Ave., downtown
Manitou Springs, Colorado
www.cograilway.com

Pinecrest Gardens
11000 Red Rd.
Corner of SW 111th St. (Killian Dr.)
    and SW 57th Ave. (Red Rd.)
Pinecrest, Florida
www.pinecrest-fl.gov/gardens.htm

The Pines Cottages
346 Weaverville Highway
Asheville, North Carolina
www.ashevillepines.com

Pioneer Village
138 E. U.S. 6
Take NE 10 for 12½ miles south of I-80
    to Exit 279
Minden, Nebraska
www.pioneervillage.org

Pirate's Cove Adventure Golf
Broadway St./W 13/16 and 23
Wisconsin Dells, Wisconsin
www.piratescovewisdells.com

Pistachio Tree Ranch
7320 U.S. 70 N.
Alamogordo, New Mexico
www.PistachioTreeRanch.com

Playland (aka Rye Playland)
Playland Parkway
New England Thruway/I-95, exit 19; or Hutch-
    inson River Parkway to Cross Westchester
    Expressway/287 East; by train from NYC,
    take the New Haven Line to Rye Station,
    where bus #75 transports free to Playland
Rye, New York
www.ryeplayland.org

Pocahontas Motel
3533 U.S. 441
Cherokee, North Carolina

Powers Hamburgers
1402 S. Harrison
Fort Wayne, Indiana

Prairie Dog Town
457 U.S. 83
I-70, Exit 70
Oakley, Kansas

Prehistoric Forest
36848 U.S. 101
South of Humbug Mountain State Park
Port Orford, Oregon

The striking Rest Haven sign in Springfield, Missouri, was reportedly the inspiration for the better-known Munger Moss sign in nearby Lebanon.

Professor Cline's Haunted Monster Museum
Dinosaur Kingdom
U.S. 11
I-81, Exit 175
Natural Bridge, Virginia
www.naturalbridgeva.com/monster.html

Ralph's Muffler and Brake Shops
1250 W. 16th St.
Indianapolis, Indiana

Ranch Store Gift Shop
Badlands Loop Rd./SD 240
I-90, Exit 131, just over 1 mile south toward
    the eastern end of Badlands National Park
Cactus Flat, South Dakota

Red Caboose Getaway
24 Old Coyote Way
Two hours west of Seattle on the Olympic
    Peninsula, off U.S. 101
Sequim, Washington
www.redcaboosegetaway.com

Red Caboose Motel and Restaurant
312 Paradise Lane
Near PA 741, 7 miles south of U.S. 30
Strasburg, Pennsylvania
www.redcaboosemotel.com

Red's
Main St. & Water St.
Wiscasset, Maine

Redwood Tree Service Station
859 State St. N.
Ukiah, California

Reed's Standard Service Station, Niland's Café,
    and Colo Motel
24 Lincoln Way/230th St.
Immediately west of U.S. 65
Colo, Iowa

Rest Haven Court
2000 E. Kearney St.
Springfield, Missouri

Ripley's Davy Crockett Mini Golf
U.S. 441 Parkway, traffic light #1
Gatlinburg, Tennessee

Roadside America
I-78, Exit 23
Shartlesville, Pennsylvania
www.roadsideamericainc.com

Rock Café
114 W. Main St.
Stroud, Oklahoma
www.rockcaferoute66.com

Rock City Gardens
1400 Patten Rd.
On Lookout Mountain, 6 miles from downtown
    Chattanooga, Tennessee
Lookout Mountain, Georgia
www.seerockcity.com

Rose Service Station
Old Knoxville Rd. just off Dixie Highway/U.S. 25 E.
Tazewell, Tennessee
www.claibornecounty.com/tazgulfstation.htm

Classic souvenirs at South of the Border.

Rosie's Diner
1400 14 Mile Rd. NE/M-57
1 mile east of U.S. 131, Exit 101
Rockford, Michigan
www.rosiesdiner.com

Route 66 Gift Shop and Museum
217 E. Route 66
Seligman, Arizona
ww.route66giftshop.com

Route 66 State Park
97 N. Outer Rd.
Eureka, Missouri
www.mostateparks.com/route66.htm

Roy's Café and Motel
National Old Trails Highway
Amboy, California
www.rt66roys.com

St. Augustine Alligator Farm
999 Anastasia Blvd./A1A
South of downtown, west of Anastasia
    State Recreation Area
St. Augustine, Florida
www.alligatorfarm.com

Sandy Chanty
5457 Lake Rd. E.
Geneva-on-the-Lake, Ohio
www.sandychanty.com

Santa Cruz Beach Boardwalk
400 Beach St.
Santa Cruz, California
www.BeachBoardwalk.com

Santa's Land Park and Zoo
571 Wolfetown Rd./U.S. 19
Cherokee, North Carolina
www.santaslandnc.com

Santa's Village
528 Presidential Highway/U.S. 2 W.
Jefferson, New Hampshire
www.santasvillage.com

Santa's Village fan site
Formerly in East Dundee, Illinois
www.santasvillage.net
www.groups.msn.com/santasvillage

Santa's Workshop
U.S. 24 west of Manitou Springs
North Pole, Colorado
www.santas-colo.com

Santa's Workshop
Whiteface Mountain Memorial
    Highway/NY 431
1 1/2 miles west of Wilmington
    and NY 86
North Pole, New York
www.northpoleny.com

Santa Fe Villas and Social Service Center
(former Alamo Plaza Hotel)
2370 Metropolitan Pkwy. SW
Near intersection of I-78, I-85, and
   Langford Pkwy.
Atlanta, Georgia

Satellite Motel
6006 L St./U.S. 275
At intersection with S. 60th St.
I-80, Exit 450
Omaha, Nebraska
www.satellitemotelomaha.com

Scenic Motel
3941 Parkway/U.S. 441 and U.S. 321
Pigeon Forge, Tennessee

Sears Motel and Campground
1023 MT 49 N.
^{1}/2 mile north of U.S. 2
East Glacier Park, Montana
www.searsmotel.com

Shady Dell RV Park
1 Old Douglas Rd.
Intersection of AZ 92 and AZ 80
Bisbee, Arizona
www.theshadydell.com

Shankweiler's Drive-In Theatre
4540 Shankweiler Rd.
Orefield, Pennsylvania
Just off PA 309, 4 miles north of U.S. 22,
   northwest of Allentown
www.shankweilers.com

Shell Factory and Nature Park
2787 North Tamiami Trail/Bus. U.S. 41
Sign along N. Cleveland Ave/U.S. 41
North Fort Myers, Florida
www.shellfactory.com

Shell gas station
Preservation North Carolina
Sprague St. and Peachtree St.
Winston-Salem, North Carolina
www.oldgas.com/info/ws_shell.htm

Shepherd of the Hills Homestead
5586 W. MO 76
Branson, Missouri
www.oldmatt.com

Sherman Perk
Former Copeland Service Station
4924 W. Roosevelt Dr.
Milwaukee, Wisconsin
www.wisconsinhistory.org/hp/buildings/
   restorations/copeland.asp

Showtown Restaurant and Lounge
10901 U.S. 41 N.
Gibsontown, Florida

Signal Station Pizza
8302 N. Lombard St./U.S. 30
At N. Charleston Ave. near the St. Johns Bridge
Portland, Oregon

Silver Dollar City
399 Indian Point Rd.
West of town along MO 76
Branson, Missouri
www.silverdollarcity.com

Six Gun City
U.S. 2 E.
Jefferson, New Hampshire
www.sixguncity.com

66 Drive-In Theater
17231 Old 66 Blvd.
Carthage, Missouri
www.66drivein.com

Sleepy Hollow Motel
94 E. Main St./UT19
Green River, Utah

Slovak Folk Crafts
1605 S. Center St./PA 208
I-79, exit 113, just east of outlet stores
Grove City, Pennsylvania
www.slovakfolkcrafts.com

Snow Cap Drive-In
301 E. Chino Ave.
Seligman, Arizona

Soco Crafts and Tower
6638 Soco Rd./U.S. 19
Maggie Valley, North Carolina

South Dakota's Original 1880 Town
Box 507
22 miles west of Murdo, just off I-90 at Exit 170
Murdo, South Dakota
www.1880town.com

South of the Border
U.S. 301 and 501
I-95, Exit 193
Dillon, South Carolina
www.pedroland.com

Spook Hill
Near North Ave.
Lake Wells, Florida

Sport Center Arcade
5438 Lake Rd. E.
Geneva-on-the-Lake, Ohio

Standin' on the Corner Park
2nd St./old U.S. 66 at Kinsley Ave.
Winslow, Arizona
www.standinonthecorner.com

Star Drive-In and Best Western Movie Manor
2830 W. U.S. 160
2¹/₂ miles west of Monte Vista toward Durango
Monte Vista, Colorado
www.bestlodging.com/sites4/43849/index.shtml

Steak 'n Shake
1158 E. St. Louis St.
Springfield, Missouri
www.steaknshake.com/history.asp

Stewart's Petrified Wood
I-40 E.
Holbrook, Arizona
www.petrifiedwood.com

Stonehenge
University of Missouri–Rolla
Bishop Ave./Loop 44/U.S. 63 at bend near
    St. Patrick's Lane
Rolla, Missouri
www.web.umr.edu/~stonehen

Stonehenge
Maryhill Museum of Art
35 Maryhill Museum Dr.
Goldendale, Washington
www.maryhillmuseum.org/about.htm

Story Land
Route 16
Glen, New Hampshire
www.storylandnh.com

Suncoast Primate Sanctuary
    (currently not open to the public)
Formerly Chimp Farm
4600 Alt. U.S. 19
Just south of Tarpon Springs
Palm Harbor, Florida
www.suncoastprimates.org

Sunken Gardens
1825 Fourth St. N.
St. Petersburg, Florida
www.stpete.org/fun/parks/sunken.htm

Sunnyside Pool, Pavilion, and Cafe
1755 Lake Shore Blvd. W. at Parkside Dr.
Toronto, Canada
www.torontobeach.ca/beaches/beach.jsp?id=3
For more on park history, visit
    www.cec.chebucto.org/ClosPark/
    SunnSide.html

Swap Shop Drive-In Theatre
3291 W. Sunrise Blvd.
Between I-95 and the Florida Turnpike, just
    northwest of downtown
Fort Lauderdale, Florida
www.floridaswapshop.com

Sylvan Beach Amusement Park
Between Syracuse and Utica on the eastern shore
   of Oneida Lake; New York Thruway/I-90, Exit
   34, go north on NY 13 about 7 miles
Sylvan Beach, New York
www.sylvanbeach.org/amusementpark

Tangletown Gardens
5353 Nicollet Ave. S.
Minneapolis, Minnesota
www.tangletowngardens.com

Tee Pee Curios
924 E. Route 66
Tucumcari, New Mexico

Tee Pee Motel
1.2 miles south of Highway 59 on Bus. 59
Wharton, Texas
www.teepeemotel.bravehost.com

Teepee Trading Post
Grant Rd., I-40 Exit 359 at the New Mexico
   border
Lupton, Arizona

Three Bears Gift Shop
2850 Parkway, U.S. 441
Pigeon Forge, Tennessee
www.pigeon-forge-attractions.com

Timbavati Wildlife Park at Storybook Gardens
1500 Wisconsin Dells Parkway/U.S. 12
Next to Noah's Ark
Wisconsin Dells, Wisconsin
www.timbavati.net
www.storybookgardens.net/storybook.html

The Timber Lodge
3627 W. Colorado Ave.
Colorado Springs, Colorado
www.timberlodge.pikes-peak.com

Time Square
5465 Lake Rd. E.
Geneva-on-the-Lake, Ohio

Tinkertown Museum
121 Sandia Crest Rd.
20 minutes northeast of Albuquerque
   on NM 536
Sandia Park, New Mexico
www.tinkertown.com

Tiny Town
6249 S. Turkey Creek Rd.
5 miles west of the C-470 and U.S. 285
   interchange, southwest of Denver
Morrison, Colorado
www.tinytownrailroad.com

Tommy Bartlett Exploratory
560 Wisconsin Dells Parkway
Wisconsin Dells, Wisconsin
www.tommybartlett.com

Tonga Room and Hurricane Bar
Fairmount Hotel
950 Mason St.
San Francisco, California
www.fairmont.com/sanfrancisco

Totem Pole Park
4 miles east of town on OK 28A
Foyil, Oklahoma
www.rchs1.org/totem.htm

Tour-Thru Tree
CA 169
$1/4$ mile east of U.S. 101
Klamath, California

Tower Station and U-Drop-Inn
Route 66 at U.S. 83
Shamrock, Texas

Town-N-Country Cottages
123 Crystal Park Rd.
Manitou Springs, Colorado
www.townncountryc.com

Trees of Mystery
15500 Highway 101 N.
Klamath, California
www.treesofmystery.net

Triple XXX Family Restaurant
2 N. Salisbury St.
West Lafayette, Indiana
www.triplexxxfamilyrestaurant.com

Union Station, a Wyndham Historic Hotel
1001 Broadway
Nashville, Tennessee
www.historichotels.org/hotel/291

Van's Pig Stands Bar-B-Q Restaurant
320 N. Porter/old U.S. 77
I-35, Robinson Street exit
Norman, Oklahoma
www.pigstands.com

Van's Pig Stands Bar-B-Q Restaurant
717 E. Highland
I-40, Harrison St., Exit 186
Shawnee, Oklahoma
www.pigstands.com

The Varsity Athens
1000 W. Broad St.
Athens, Georgia

The Varsity Downtown
61 North Ave.
Across the I-75/85 connector from Georgia Tech
Atlanta, Georgia
www.thevarsity.com

The Varsity Jr.
1085 Lindbergh Dr.
Atlanta, Georgia

Vista Drive-In
1911 Tuttle Creek Blvd./U.S. 24
Manhattan, Kansas
www.vistadrivein.com

Wagon Wheel Restaurant
2755 Wagon Wheel Rd.
Oxnard, California

Waimea Valley Audubon Center
59-864 Kamehameha Highway/HI 83
North shore of Oahu across from Waimea Bay
Haleiwa, Hawaii
www.audubon.org/local/sanctuary/Brochures/
    Waimea.html

Waldameer Park
220 Peninsula Dr./PA 832 at the entrance
    to Presque Isle
Erie, Pennsylvania
www.waldameer.com

Wall Drug
510 Main St.
I-90 Exit 110 near Badlands National Park,
    50 miles east of Rapid City
Wall, South Dakota
www.WallDrug.com

Watts Towers
1765 E. 107th St.
Los Angeles, California
www.wattstowers.us

Wave Organ
Exploratorium at the Palace of Fine Arts
3601 Lyon St.
Off U.S. 101 near the Golden Gate Bridge
San Francisco, California
www.exploratorium.edu/visit/wave_organ.html

"You say that man with a gun is your sweetheart?!" One of the many attractions at Wall Drug in South Dakota.

White Turkey Drive-in
388 E. Main Rd./U.S. 20
Conneaut, Ohio
www.whiteturkey.8k.com

Wigwam Motel
811 W. Hopi Dr.
Holbrook, Arizona
www.galerie-kokopelli.com/wigwam

Wigwam Motel
2728 W. Foothill Blvd./Historic Route 66
I-215, exit W. 6th Street, then go west on 5th St
Or I-10, exit Pepper Ave. and go north
Rialto, California
www.wigwammotel.com

Wigwam Village
811 W. Hopi Dr.
Holbrook, Arizona
www.galerie-kokopelli.com/wigwam

Wigwam Village #2
601 N. Dixie Highway/U.S. 31 W.
I-65, Exit 53 to KY 90 E., then north on 31 W.
Cave City, Kentucky
www.wigwamvillage.com

Wild West City
Route 206
I-80, Exit 25, then take Route 206 north to
   Lackawanna Dr. and turn right
Netcong, New Jersey
www.wildwestcity.com

Willow Creek–China Flat Museum
Highway 299 and Highway 96
Willow Creek, California
www.bfro.net/NEWS/wcmuseum.htm

Wisconsin Concrete Park
WI 13
1 mile south of town
Phillip, Wisconsin
www.friendsoffredsmith.org

Of the thousands of offbeat attractions on RoadsideAmerica.com that we've investigated, we recall most clearly the funkier, less safety-proofed destinations—ones where we almost died. Or could have died. Or at least thought, "It would be embarrassing to die here!" Whether it was the Fire-Guns-for-Five-Bucks guy swiveling his fifty caliber in the wrong direction, the crawl through the giant hollow Christian cross arm eighty feet off of the ground with the homeboy hole in the floor or the man with the Museum of Menstruation in his basement who smiled a little too much, the memories are deep-fried into our brains.

Which brings us to Bayou Bob's Rattlesnake Ranch in Santo, Texas. Just back from turtle-trapping in the swamp, Bob cheerfully welcomed us one summer night, his head and T-shirt drenched in sweat. We stepped into his building and up on to an odd, wobbly wooden floor, our nostrils suddenly assaulted by a bitter smell. Scores of snake skins dangled like stalactites, drying on the walls. The room was filled with a steady hiss, like an overtaxed air conditioning system. Except it wasn't.

It was rattlesnakes—hundreds of them—and they were beneath us in wooden boxes that we belatedly realized made up the floor on which we were standing. Bob popped the hatch on a rickety container clogged with writhing snakes and gleefully lifted a five-foot rattler with a short pole. As it wriggled loose and dropped out of our camera frames, Bayou Bob assured us snake bites are rarely fatal. You're only in trouble, he told us, if you get bitten in the face, "where all those blood vessels are."

—DOUG KIRBY, KEN SMITH, and MIKE WILKINS,
   editors of RoadsideAmerica.com and authors of
   Roadside America and *New Roadside America*

Wonderland Amusement Park
2601 Dumas Dr.
Along U.S. 87 N at Thompson Park
Amarillo, Texas
www.wonderlandpark.com

Our favorite roadside attractions are the ones that make you scratch your head and wonder why someone would take the time and effort to produce something so strange. These sites are often not on any tourist maps, and it's difficult to find their origins, as they weren't made to attract tourists, but rather they just happened.

The sites we're talking about are America's walls of gum. These strange roadside phenomena can be found in various states and anyone can add to them. One gum wall is at the Pike Place Market Theater in Seattle, Washington. Around 1990, patrons waiting in line decided to stick their used gum on a fifteen foot wall. Today, gum sculptures and gum names cover it entirely.

Bubble Gum Alley is located off of Broad Street in San Luis Obispo, California. It was created in 1960 by unknown chewers. Legend has it that the students of nearby Cal Poly were the ones that started it all. Today, both sides of the alley are affixed with wads of gum. Some go as far as to spell out declarations of love, and some even leave their business cards.

The Maid Rite Sandwich Shop in Greenville, Ohio, must have some tasty sandwiches, leading their customers (drive-up and dine-in alike) to drool and loose their gum. How else can you explain the fact that customers routinely take chewed-up gum and stick it onto the outside of the building? The entire exterior of the shop is covered with wads of gum. The owner claims it was started in the 1950s, and as much as they tried to clean the gum off, patrons still keep sticking it back on. This less-than-appetizing display, however, doesn't seem to keep sandwich-lovers away.

—MARK SCEURMAN and MARK MORAN, Weird U.S., www.weirdus.com

Mark Moran and Mark Sceurman at The Maid Rite's famous Wall Of Gum. DAN WALWORTH

World's Largest Ball of Twine
Ball of Twine Souvenir and Gift Shop in the Great
   Plains Art and Antique Gallery
Wisconsin St./U.S. 24
Cawker City, Kansas
www.skyways.lib.ks.us/towns/Cawker/twine.html
www.theballotwine.com

World's Largest Twine Ball by One Man
1st St./C.R. 14
Darwin, Minnesota

Wright's Dairy Rite
346 Greenville Ave./U.S. 11
I-81, Exit 222
Staunton, Virginia
www.Dairy-Rite.com

Ye Olde Curiosity Shop
1001 Alaskan Way/WA 519
Pier 54 on Puget Sound, near Madison St.
   and Spring St.
Seattle, Washington
www.yeoldecuriosityshop.com

FURTHER READING AND SURFING

BOOKS

Allan Herschell Co. *Kiddielands . . . A Business with a Future.* North Tonawanda, NY: Allan Herschell, c. 1956.

Ant Farm. *Automerica: A Trip Down U.S. Highways from World War II to the Future.* New York: Dutton, 1976.

Baeder, John. *Gas, Food, and Lodging: A Postcard Odyssey, Through the Great American Roadside.* New York: Abbeville Press, 1982.

Butko, Brian. *Greetings from the Lincoln Highway: America's First Coast-to-Coast Road.* Mechanicsburg, PA: Stackpole Books, 2005.

Butko, Brian, and Sarah Butko. *Roadside Giants.* Mechanicsburg, PA: Stackpole Books, 2005.

Butko, Brian, and Kevin Patrick. *Diners of Pennsylvania.* Mechanicsburg, PA: Stackpole Books, 1999.

Friedman, Jan. *Eccentric America.* Guilford, CT: Bradt, 2004.

Futrell, Jim. *Amusement Parks of New Jersey.* Mechanicsburg, PA: Stackpole Books, 2004.

———. *Amusement Parks of New York.* Mechanicsburg, PA: Stackpole Books, 2006.

———. *Amusement Parks of Pennsylvania.* Mechanicsburg, PA: Stackpole Books, 2002.

Garbin, Randy. *Diners of New England.* Mechanicsburg, Pa.: Stackpole Books, 2005.

Genovese, Peter. *Roadside Florida: The Definitive Guide to the Kingdom of Kitsch.* Mechanicsburg, Pa.: Stackpole Books, 2006.

Gutman, Richard J. S. *American Diner: Then and Now.* New York: HarperPerennial, 1993.

Hastings, Kirk. *Doo Wop Motels: Architectural Treasures of The Wildwoods.* Mechanicsburg, PA: Stackpole Books, 2007.

Hollis, Tim. *From Dixie to Disney: 100 Years of Roadside Fun.* Jackson: University Press of Mississippi, 1999.

———. *Glass Bottom Boats and Mermaid Tails: Florida's Tourist Springs.* Mechanicsburg, PA.: Stackpole Books, 2006.

Jakle, John A., Keith A. Sculle, and Jefferson C. Rogers. *The Motel in America.* Baltimore: Johns Hopkins University Press, 1996.

Jensen, Jamie. *Road Trip USA.* Emeryville, CA: Avalon, 2006.

Knowles, Drew. *Route 66 Adventure Handbook.* Expanded 3rd ed. Santa Monica, CA: Santa Monica Press, 2006.

Kirby, Doug, Ken Smith, and Mike Wilkins. *The New Roadside America.* New York: Fireside, 1992.

Krim, Arthur. *Route 66: Iconography of the American Highway.* Santa Fe, NM: Center for American Places, 2006.

Langdon, Philip. *Orange Roofs, Golden Arches: The Architecture of American Chain Restaurants.* New York: Knopf, 1986.

Liebs, Chester. *Main Street to Miracle Mile: American Roadside Architecture.* Baltimore: Johns Hopkins University Press, 1995.

Margolies, John. *The End of the Road.* New York: Penguin, 1981.

———. *Fun along the Road: American Roadside Attractions.* New York: Bulfinch Press, 1998.

McClanahan, Jerry. *The EZ66 Guide for Travelers*. Lake Arrowhead, CA: National Historic Route 66 Federation, 2005.

Moran, Mark, and Mark Sceurman. *Weird U.S.* New York: Barnes and Noble, 2004.

Peterson, Eric. *Roadside Americana*. Lincolnwood, IL: Publications International, 2004.

Pomeroy, Earl. *In Search of the Golden West: The Tourist in Western America*. New York: Knopf, 1957.

Stern, Jane, and Michael Stern. *Amazing America*. New York: Random House, 1977.

———. *Two for the Road: Our Love Affair with American Food*. Boston: Houghton Mifflin, 2006.

Stern, Jerome. *Florida Dreams*. Tallahassee: Florida State University Gallery and Museum, 1993.

Walker, Harry M. *Wacky & Wonderful Roadside Attractions of Alaska*. Kenmore, Washington: Epicenter Press, 2002.

Wallis, Michael. *Route 66: The Mother Road*. New York: St. Martin's, 1990.

Witzel, Michael Karl. *The American Motel*. Osceola, WI: MBI, 2000.

WEBSITES

www.bluemaumau.org/history_of_franchising
Blue MauMau is building a comprehensive history of franchising.

www.bygonebyways.com
Bygone Byways has astounding roadside images, especially from the Southwest.

www.cr.nps.gov/rt66
The National Park Service Route 66 Corridor Preservation Program

www.dreamscape.com/dbporter/wigwam_nation.htm
This site lists dozens of wigwam structures, past and present.

www.eccentricamerica.com
Website of Jan Friedman, author of *Eccentric America*.

www.highwayhost.org/AlamoPlaza/alamoplaza1.htm
Alamo Plaza history by Richard Kummerlowe

www.historic101.com
Don Wilson's Highway 101 Project.

www.johnbaeder.com
Website of the author-artist John Baeder.

www.johnmargolies.com
Tons of photographs by John Margolies.

www.mockturtlepress.com
American Road magazine covers roads and things along them.

www.roadsideamerica.com
The most popular guide to unusual attractions.

www.roadsidefans.com
Glenn Wells runs the Roadside Fans yahoo group and this website.

Route40.net
Frank Brusca's ode to the famed transcontinental highway.

www.route66news.org
A terrific roundup of Route 66 news by Ron Warnick.

www.theamericanroadside.com
Ron Dylewski's roundup of roadside-related news.

www.tunneltree.com/tunneltree/tunneltree.html
Drive-through tree postcards, photos, and stereoviews.

www.narrowlarry.com/page1.html
Narrow Larry's list of visionary folk-art environments in the United States.

www.theimaginaryworld.com/PARKS1.html
A great compilation of Story Book Lands.

ACKNOWLEDGMENTS

Editor Kyle Weaver once again helped us in too many ways to count. Also at Stackpole, we appreciate the hard work of copyeditor Joyce Bond, managing editor Amy Cooper, production manager Cathy Craley, proofreader Linda Dalton, paginator Kerry Jean Handel, designer Beth Oberholtzer, and art director Caroline Stover. We also give a huge thank you to all the contributors to this book for their stories, photos, and support. Some who helped but whose names don't appear elsewhere include JoAnn Adams, Carol Ahlgren, Michael "Bert" Bedeau, Valentine and Cassie Brkich, Kevin and Lori Butko, Tina Emery, Mike Engle, Michael Houser, Rich Kummerlowe, Jay and Joyce Link, Lester Link, Ralph Link, Debrean and Randy Loy, Mary Beth Miller, Michael and Karen O'Dea, Robert and Chelsea O'Dea, Clarissa Perez, Debbie and Don Pipp, Erika Provance, April Reading, Gregory Smith, and Phyllis and Rick Wilson.

They're proud of their potatoes in Blackfoot, Idaho. KEVIN PATRICK

INDEX